VOLUME TWO
AN IRREVERENT LOOK AT SIXTYISH AND SINGLE

Susan Luzader
Illustrated by Claire Luzader

Black Rose Writing | Texas

©2024 by Susan Luzader
All rights reserved. No part of this book may be reproduced, stored in a retrieval system or transmitted in any form or by any means without the prior written permission of the publishers, except by a reviewer who may quote brief passages in a review to be printed in a newspaper, magazine or journal.

The author grants the final approval for this literary material.

First printing

This is a work of fiction. Names, characters, businesses, places, events, and incidents are either the products of the author's imagination or used in a fictitious manner. Any resemblance to actual persons, living or dead, or actual events is purely coincidental.

ISBN: 978-1-68513-509-6
PUBLISHED BY BLACK ROSE WRITING
www.blackrosewriting.com

Printed in the United States of America
Suggested Retail Price (SRP) $17.95 USD

Wine and Cereal: Volume Two is printed in Minion Pro

*As a planet-friendly publisher, Black Rose Writing does its best to eliminate unnecessary waste to reduce paper usage and energy costs, while never compromising the reading experience. As a result, the final word count vs. page count may not meet common expectations.

For my brother, Tom

Acknowledgements

This book would not have been possible without the unrelenting optimism, energy, and spreadsheets of my publicist, Ann Boland.

Thank you, Tom Cheknis and Norah White, for your expertise and enthusiasm.

Harvey Sam, at Simutek Computers, saved this manuscript from oblivion.

Thank you, Billy L., for all the stories.

My writing group, Susan Smith (*My Heart Attack Saved My Life ... But for What?)* and Pamela Hale Trachta (*Flying Lessons*), are the epitome of Fabulous Women!

My sons, Justin and Steven, fill my heart with humor and love.

As always, my rascals, Seth, Bailey, Jackson, Tristan, and Hunter, inspire and entertain me.

Pip and Oscar, the knuckleheads, alert me to barbarians at the gate and javelina at the French doors.

Preface

Why *Wine and Cereal*? It's one of the questions I'm asked when discussing my book.

When I took the first feeble steps in my new single life, I was often fueled with cereal straight from the box. It was easy; it was filling. Of course, as anyone in my family will tell you, there was always wine.

My friend, Gary Wagnon, suggested the title when I began my first blog posts. Thank you, Gary!

What Wine Goes with Cheerios?

It's 5:30 on a Tuesday night and I'm facing the age-old question of the Suddenly Single. What wine goes with Cheerios? Everyone knows you only serve white with a fruit-based cereal, such as Raisin Bran. But Cheerios? That's another matter altogether.

"I'm not falling into that trap," a Suddenly Single friend told me over dinner in an Italian restaurant. "I'm not eating cereal or crackers and cheese for dinner. I'm just not."

I look down at the yellow box and sigh. I still cook for sick friends, and I bake cookies for the grandkids, but otherwise, my gorgeous five-burner Wolf stove sits idle. One morning, I woke to find half a roach, legs up, next to one burner. I shudder to think where the other half might be. I check my Cheerios carefully before I eat them.

"When you begin to eat frozen dinners—and you will," my mother tells me, "I suggest Stouffer's. They're the best." She's the veteran of two divorces and has been single for twenty-five years.

Of course, I can't eat frozen dinners now and admit she was right. So I graze throughout the kitchen like a goat foraging for just the right morsel in a well-trodden field. I'm still a goat, I tell myself. I'm still a domesticated animal. I haven't gone completely feral. Yet.

I open the refrigerator one more time, hoping the answer to my question will appear to me in a sudden flash of insight. Then it does. Tucked behind bottles of water and cans of dog food is a half-full bottle of pinot noir. Of course, I realize, the answer was here all along. What wine goes with Cheerios? All of them.

VOLUME TWO
AN IRREVERENT LOOK AT SIXTYISH AND SINGLE

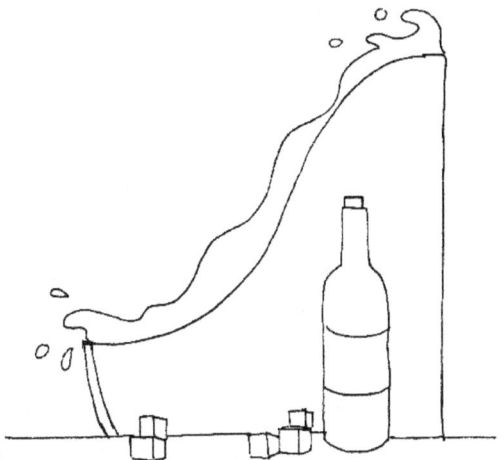

Girls Just Want to Have Fun

"You know," my son says, "you're kind of a cross between Cyndi Lauper and Chuck Norris."

We are discussing costumes for my daughter-in-law's 40th birthday party with a 1980s theme. I agree with my son but can't see myself in a beard, so I'll go as Cyndi.

"Who's Cyndi Lauper?" my granddaughter asks.

The night of the party, I slip on some tights, tease my hair, don a sassy t-shirt, and drape myself in colorful beads. *I'm looking good*, I think. Then I look in the mirror. I should have gone as Chuck Norris.

"You look pretty," my granddaughter says. If by pretty, she means I look like a Cyndi who has eaten her way through a series of breakfast buffets followed by a string of frat parties, she would be correct.

Cyndi does not deserve this. My *True Colors* appear to have been run through a blender. I try to remember if Cyndi ever wore an overcoat.

My granddaughter drags me downstairs, and I realize I am the oldest person there—by about 20 years. I am surrounded by punk rockers, Madonnas, Jedi knights, and even a Gordon Gecko. They look fabulous. I look as if poor Cyndi spent her life eating Hostess Twinkies and drinking cheap rum.

I hear shouts and laughter outside and discover guests crowded around an ice sculpture shaped like a luge. Liquor bottles surround the ice.

I watch as one of my sons places his mouth at the bottom of the ice luge. My other son pours a shot of tequila from the top. Everyone whoops and laughs as the tequila slides into his mouth.

"What about germs?" I ask. These lovely young people turn to look at me as if I have a ski pole sticking out of my head.

"What the ice doesn't kill, the alcohol will," my son, the doctor, says as he wobbles back into the house.

"C'mon, Mom!" yells my other son. "It's your turn!"

I shake my head and try to duck back inside. The crowd chants, "Nana! Nana! Nana!"

What would Cyndi do?

"Only wine!" I shout at the crowd. "Just one shot of wine!"

I position myself and open my mouth. Cameras click all around me. Everyone wants a photo of the old broad doing an ice luge.

The wine tastes sharp and cold as it zips into my mouth. "One more!" the crowd chants. I'm pretty sure the winemaker never intended his vintage to be consumed down an ice luge, but I take another shot.

"That was cool, Mom," my son says.

I giggle. "Let's face it *Girls Just Want to Have Fun!*"

Bright Lights, Big City

I charge up the entry stairs to New York's Museum of Modern Art and stop at a painting of people being shot to death. Men, women, and even a baby scream in terror as a hand holding a gun mows them down.

Good Morning, New York City!

"Never hang your purse on the back of your chair in a restaurant," one of our guides instructs, "not even in the nicest places."

Bright lights, big city, *indeed*.

I'm here with twenty other folks to see five Broadway plays in six nights. Our tour leader is a professor emeritus of theater. He must be a *very* good actor because he acts like he loves being asked stupid questions—mostly from me.

We clump together like ducklings as we wander the streets, looking up at magnificent architecture and down at squashed donuts and dog poop. Not everyone scoops.

We ride carriages in Central Park, ride the subway with patient commuters, ride in taxis that smell like someone *has* scooped and left it in the cab.

We buy $5 umbrellas and run laughing through the rain after a show.

We desert dwellers learn to push through crowds toward our destination and to open our bags for inspection before entering every building.

We watch the best theater in the world and some of the worst. We dissect them all in the hotel bar, pretending we are sophisticated and urbane. The waiters treat us with disdain, and we act like we don't care.

The Metropolitan Museum of Art (we fancy folk simply call it The Met) soothes us with European art and sculpture. We turn the corner and walk straight into a gallery featuring Camp. We peer at Oscar Wilde's velvet capes, Liberace's sequins, and David Bowie's Ziggy Stardust.

I discover I love Camp, even though I can't define it. I have a sudden urge to dress like Cher. Where's Bob Mackie when you need him?

One night, we are the last to leave the hotel bar. I have never in my life closed *a bar*.

Our tour guides arch their eyebrows at us as we stumble into the conference room the next morning, clutching coffee and asking if anyone has an aspirin. I cannot *wait* to go again.

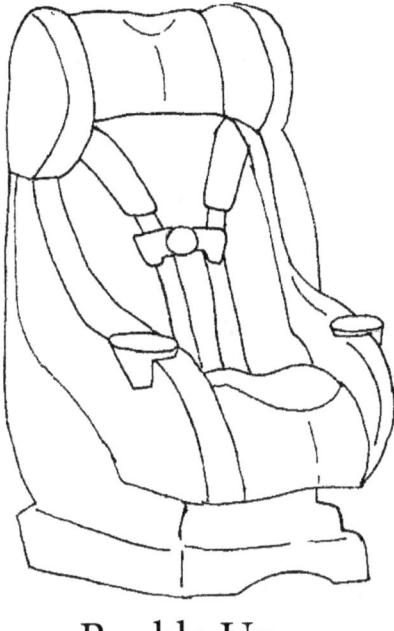

Buckle Up

"I *know* how to buckle a car seat," I tell my son. "This is my fourth grandchild. I *understand* about car seats."

My ever-patient son sighs and backs away. I glare at him as I fasten my grandson into his car seat.

I drive off, my head in the air and my grandson safely in his car seat. I mutter to myself about ungrateful sons.

My grandson burbles, and I burble back. I make almost every green light, which I'm sure is a good omen. I pull into our first stop, the pet store. I hop out and open the passenger door, causing my grandson to giggle and smile.

"Let's get you out of that seat," I chatter, like the fool I am. I pause, squinting at the harness. It doesn't look quite right. I panic for a second, thinking it is unsafe, but my grandson is safely, tightly, *very, very tightly*, strapped into his seat. The poor child can barely move. Mummies had looser bindings than his.

Squinting again, I realize in my haste to show proficiency, I turned the release buckle upside down. My grandson reaches for me, expecting to be freed.

No problem, I think. I can reach under and release the catch. I snake my thumb under the buckle. I press. I press hard. Nothing happens. My grandson looks puzzled. He reaches for me again.

"Just a minute, sweet baby," I say more confidently than I feel. I tightened the straps so much that my knobby, arthritic fingers can't quite get a grip. I begin to sweat.

A button, I think. There must be a button to loosen the straps. I crawl into the car, running my hand along the back, sides, and front of the seat. My grandson has ceased to burble and is considering screaming about his continued incarceration.

I sweat more.

I sing to keep my grandson from screaming. I pressed the release button so much and so hard, my thumbs begin to swell.

I realize I spent the last few minutes with my hands buried in my grandson's diaper area. Now I look around, hoping no one will see me and think I'm a pervert.

Explorers on the Amazon did not sweat as much as I'm sweating. I panic and call my daughter-in-law. Luckily for my dignity, she is swimming laps and does not answer.

As my fingers search the car seat for a hundredth time, I find the instruction book tucked into the bottom. I flip it open. There it is, the release button—right next to the strap I used to tighten the harness.

Freeing my grandson, I hug him to my sweaty chest. We finish our errands and return home.

"So," my son says as he helps me unload the car. "How did it go?"

"No problem," I say. "No problem at all."

Hell Bound

With apologies to Dante's Inferno

"I have a therapist," my date says. *TMI*, I think for a first date.

My date tells me he once met his therapist on an online dating site *before* she became his therapist.

Ah, I realize, I have entered the spiraling pit of dating hell. Dante's *Inferno* has nine circles—I hope dating hell has far fewer. This fellow has skipped right over Circles One through Three and gone straight to Four.

"Do you think I should tell my therapist? That we've met online?" And here we are at Circle Five.

"I certainly understand why you would need a therapist," I say. Where is that waiter with our food? The sooner I eat, the sooner I can ditch this bozo. "I'm sure you're still grieving for your wife."

"I'm over that," the date says. "I was seeing a woman. She broke my heart." He looks like he's going to cry.

Please, please, I pray, *do not let him talk about her.*

"My therapist says," the date continues. Circle Six, here I come. "At least this proves," the date continues, "that I still have a heart that can be broken."

I try to smile, while my mind is screaming, "Run! Run fast! Run hard!"

Where is the darn waiter?

The food arrives just as he's telling me they dated for nine weeks. "She cooked breakfast for my birthday. She needed more eggs."

"My, this salad looks delicious," I desperately try.

"While I was at the store, I checked her dating account. She was online, talking with another guy." Now I think he really is going to cry.

I dig into my food. I deserve to at least get a decent meal out of this.

"I guess I shouldn't be telling you all this," he says, trying to make puppy eyes.

Dude, I think, *no one wants to hear this. No one.*

He prattles on, using the phrase *She broke my heart* at least twice more.

That's it, he's done it. He's dropped me firmly into Circle Nine. They'll have to send in search-and-rescue to find me after this.

"Would you care for dessert?" the waiter asks.

"No!" I practically scream and throw my credit card at him.

"I'd like to see you again," the date says. The only place I want to see *him* is in my rearview mirror.

I bolt for the car, no longer caring if I'm being polite. I drive as if the hounds of hell are on my tail.

Suddenly, a Baskin Robbins appears just ahead. Taking a long, slow bite of mocha chip, I begin to quench the fires of dating hell. No more, I tell myself, no more dating.

My phone pings. It's Paul, that cute fellow I met last weekend at a charity event. *Maybe,* I decide, *dating can't be all bad.*

Out of Practice

"Why do you have such a big car?" Helga asks as I slide her walker into the cargo area. Born in Germany, her voice could make an SS officer soil his shorts.

So I can fit your walker and your pillow and your bag in it, I think.

Helga harrumphs and totters to the passenger side. Her regular ride to church is ill and I've volunteered to drive.

"I brought a stool to help you get in." I place the step stool next to her.

"I do not need a step stool!" I jump back and have an urge to salute her.

I think her regular driver is not ill but cowering in a corner somewhere drinking heavily.

"This is not the direction Carol chooses," Helga announces as I pull out of her assisted living facility.

"We can take several different routes," I say.

Helga stares straight ahead and I turn around. I feel like Poland in September 1939.

"Ah," says Pastor as I help Helga out of my too-big car. "It's the Helga and Susan show." I resist the temptation to salute him with my middle finger.

Settling Helga and her pillow in her regular pew, I tuck away the walker. I am reading the Bible passages in the service today. I whisper that I'll be back in a few moments and make my way to the pulpit.

This is my first-time reading Bible verses in front of the whole church. I practiced every day. My hands shake and I'm sweating so much I can feel it pooling in my shoes.

I manage to not mangle most of the Old Testament names and return to my seat beside Germany's answer to Genghis Khan.

As I help Helga up from the pew and make our way toward the exit, Mary touches my arm, complimenting me on my reading.

Helga watches Mary walk away. She cocks her head and looks at me. "Perhaps," she says, "it would have been better if you *practiced*."

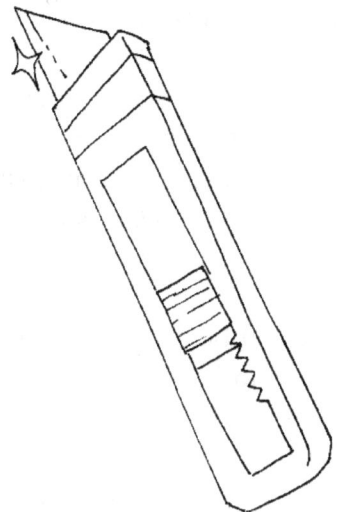

The Invisible Woman

I am FINALLY on the plane and plop into my seat, searching my pockets for the clever place where I stashed my driver's license after going through security. Touching something metal in the pocket of my puffy vest, I pull out a box cutter.

Being the fool that I am, I stare at it for a few seconds until my brain shifts into gear. *Holy %$#@!,* I almost say aloud, *I'm on an airplane and I have a box cutter in my hand!* Visions of 9/11 dance in my head.

I remember that before I left for the airport, I was cutting down boxes to put in the recycling. I left the box cutter in my vest.

My inner idiot thinks *I should tell the flight attendant that I have a box cutter.* Sometimes, I don't display the sense God gave a brick.

My next thought is *I should call my son and ask him what to do.* Because, as everyone knows, saying the words *box cutter* while sitting on a plane is the sensible course of action.

In the meantime, I'm still sitting on an airplane staring at a box cutter in my hand. I am a Sixty Something grandmother who has just watched her granddaughter dance in *The Nutcracker* (she was brilliant, by the way). I'm going to jail for the rest of my life.

The flight attendant is busy getting folks seated. The passengers mill around, stowing luggage and finding their places. And I'm still sitting on a plane with a box cutter in my hand.

I remember coming home from the Caribbean a few years before with a drug-sniffing dog searching passengers as they returned to the U.S. I stood still so the dog could have a good whiff and *they didn't even bring the dog over to sniff me!* I could have walked back into the U.S. with my pockets stuffed with cocaine, and no one would have noticed. And *I* was worried about a carved coconut souvenir.

TSA waved me through security *with a box cutter in my pocket!* I heard about this from my friends, but now I realize it is true. When you are Sixty Something, you are often invisible.

I close my fingers around the box cutter and look around. No one is pointing and screaming, "The old lady has a box cutter!" so I'm guessing my fellow passengers have not noticed it yet. Slamming my fist back into my pocket, I zip it completely and sit very, very, very still.

For the moment, I am delighted to be invisible.

The plane takes off and I relax a little. The flight attendant comes down the aisle inquiring about our beverage choices. She asks the young woman seated next to me what she would like. I prepare an answer, but she skips right over me, leaving me openmouthed and beverage-less.

Being invisible, I realize, cuts both ways.

Doggie Style

"You know," says Julia, "if your dog was human, he'd be designing women's shoes."

Julia brings her Pomeranian to dog agility events in the sidecar of her motorcycle. She is the coolest person I know, and she's *talking to me*.

She's right. Pip, my Swedish Vallhund loves his bling. His everyday collar has more studs and crystals than RuPaul's evening gown.

We're at a dog agility show in a livestock barn at the fairgrounds. It's no fit place for a dog that hates to get dirty. It's a good thing Pip doesn't have a middle finger.

In his first home, Pip was a pampered show dog who gathered blue ribbons and praise from judges. Then disaster struck—one of his testicles didn't descend. The breeder shipped him to me, where I promptly relieved him of the one remaining testicle and threw him in the agility ring. He and I have more issues than National Geographic.

"His *show* collar," Julia informs me, "is boring. He needs jewels. He needs leather. He needs *flash*."

Julia's Pomeranian sports a wide leather band with flowers and skulls and the word B****. I ask where she bought it. The Pom snaps at Pip and struts away.

I Google the name of the first site Julia mentioned, Sexy Beast. For your own protection, do *not* Google the words, *Sexy Beast*. I'm blushing just thinking about what I saw.

I'm so traumatized that I slam the computer shut and head straight for a glass or two of wine. And maybe a shot of vodka.

The next morning, Pip steps into the ring, coolly surveying the maze of jumps, tunnels, weaves, and assorted devices he must conquer to win a blue ribbon. I give him a hug and release the offending collar.

I'm running past the third or fourth obstacle before I realize Pip is not running with me. Not only is he *not* running with me, he's not even where I can see him. I whip my head around, trying to find my dog. I spot him trotting toward the judge, a large man sporting a cowboy hat and a frown.

Pip pauses, surveying the crowd and then strikes a pose—just like Madonna in *Vogue*. The cowboy definitely isn't amused and waves us out of the ring.

"Not his best effort," Julia says as I slink out of the arena. "But he did look *fabulous*."

Pig Heaven

The dogs throw themselves against the front door, tripping over each other like the Three Stooges.

It's 9 PM—bedtime for this Bonzo, a week before Christmas.

Man, I think, *this poor delivery person is running late.* The folks in the brown vans toss boxes on my porch 2-3 times a day in this season. I do love me some Amazon.

Muttering bad words, I grab my bright pink robe and march to the front door. "There better *be* something out there," I warn the dogs. They continue barking. I don't even think they notice me. They've fallen into a barking trance—like some cult that thinks it's changing the world with chanting.

Pushing my vocal hounds aside, I yank open the door, expecting to find a pile of boxes. For a moment, everything stops. The dogs freeze. I freeze. The javelina freezes, mid-chomp.

My feeble brain is having a hard time processing this Christmas tableau. Instead of Mary and Joseph, I have the remains of a Sees candy box, scattered bits of assorted chocolates, and a javelina with chocolate dripping from its jaws.

A voice at the back of my brain screams *Shut the door! Shut the door! Shut it NOW, you idiot!*

I stare at the javelina, he stares at the dogs, the dogs stare at the javelina. No one moves. Then, with a tiny *plop*, a chunk of chocolate drops from the pig's mouth onto the porch.

It's as if someone hit the fast-forward button. I scream, the javelina screams, the dogs scream as I slam the door shut.

It takes a few seconds for my brain to figure out someone delivered a box of Sees chocolate and didn't close the courtyard gate. The pig wandered in and discovered piggy heaven.

(Yes, I know they are not technically pigs, but if it looks like a duck, and quacks like a duck . . .)

I pull the door open just a crack. Mr. Javelina roots through the box, bits of cardboard and chocolate flying. Wonder if he's a mocha or a white chocolate fan? Does he prefer dark chocolate more than milk?

I let him finish his feast. It is the Christmas season, after all. He trots out the gate and I slam it shut, walking back to clean up smeared chocolate and scattered candy wrappers.

Three days later, the dogs are once more throwing themselves at the front door. I peek out and see the javelina butting his head against my gate. I know how he feels—a chocolate craving can make me slam my head against things, too.

It might be the season of giving, but I decide Santa has given the javelina enough chocolate. If any more comes, I'm keeping it for *myself*.

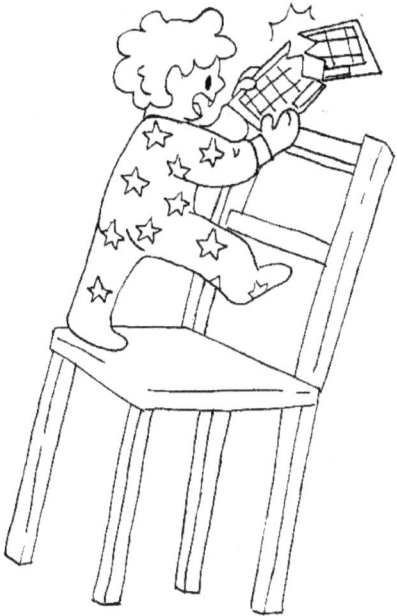

Bedlam and Boogers

Dogs bark, the baby screams, and everyone runs toward the front door. I knew Darcy was stopping by, but I am bogged down in crayons and blocks. There is drool on me, the dogs, my clothes, the floor, my hair, and possibly even on the ceiling.

I can see Darcy through the front window and she's trying to be brave. My house sounds like Bedlam on steroids. She wears a stylish ensemble. I have boogers in my ear.

I physically drag each dog toward its crate, but that doesn't stop the baying of the Baskerville hounds. By now, my grandson, The Tornado, is trying to open the front door. If he succeeds before I crate the dogs, Darcy goes down like a 98-pound weakling in front of a charging NFL tackle.

I slam the crates shut and grab The Tornado. Darcy is used to seeing me at meetings and luncheons, not covered in drool and dog hair. She takes a step back.

"Come in!" I am truly happy to see her, but I'm not sure the feeling is mutual.

"My!" she exclaims as she steps across the threshold. The big dog howls and the little one whines. The Tornado wiggles out of my grasp and streaks across the room. He returns with several crayons and what used to be a piece of paper but is now a drooly wad.

"Show me what you drew!" Darcy says, settling onto a chair after I've cleared it of several blocks, a truck, and the mangled remains of a board book. Darcy hugs him, but he dashes into the kitchen. We hear banging and slamming, and The Tornado reappears with a colander, a dented pot, and plastic containers. What used to be a pair of tongs is now a sad commentary on the strength of toddlers.

"As I was saying," Darcy begins as she pulls The Tornado onto her lap. He jumps off and shoots down the hall. I rise to give chase. "About the meeting next week..."

I pause and look back. Darcy watches me, a polite smile on her face. I realize she thinks we can have a *conversation*, an adult *conversation*. She might as well be spitting into a hurricane.

I discover my grandson banging my computer keyboard on a chair. I sweep him up and stride back to Darcy.

"Come and talk to me." Darcy leans over and beckons him. He grabs her hand, and in less than a second, it is dripping with teething drool. She hugs him, inhaling the top of his head. I get her a towel.

"I'd better be going," Darcy says as my grandson streaks back down the hall. I find him throwing tissues into the dog water.

"Precious boy," Darcy says, kissing him on the cheek. I remember her grandchildren live several states away. "Can I come back and visit him sometimes?"

"Of course," I say, struggling to keep The Tornado from shooting out the door and down the street. "But you might want to bring your own hazmat suit next time."

Car Trouble

"We'll begin slowly. Just some of the basic functions," says Cameron, the young man at the car dealership. My children have convinced me to buy a new car. This beast has so much technology that Cameron is teaching me how to start the engine. Radio stations, I fear, are beyond my grasp.

"I just don't want to cry or say bad words," I tell him as I push the start button.

"You won't," Cameron assures me. I prove him wrong within the first five minutes.

He guides me through adjusting the seat and mirrors. "Do you feel like you understand?" he asks. I nod, but I just want to go home, crawl into bed, and pull the covers over my tear-streaked face.

The car already hates me. I can sense it.

Cameron tries to teach me the navigation system. After I've pushed the wrong buttons many, many times, he sits back in the passenger seat. "Maybe," he says, "you should just use the one on your phone."

Then it's on to the radio stations. "What are your favorites?" he asks. He's forcing a smile, but I'm certain he wants to jump out of this car as much as I do.

I know I am doomed when he shows me the knob that acts like my computer mouse. "Can't I just push a button?"

"We're in the 21st century now." He's trying not to grit his teeth.

We set three stations and I'm not even sure they're the ones I usually listen to. I hope I really like the station it's on now. I can never change it.

Cameron starts to sweat.

When the machines rise, I'll be the first on their list.

"Have you shown her voice activation?" the salesman asks as he walks past.

Cameron's face drains of all color. I'm sure mine does, too.

"Why don't we set up an appointment for next week?" Cameron offers. "We can go over voice activation then."

We shake hands like two gladiators who escaped death in the ring. We agree to meet next week.

Cameron and I know I'll cancel it.

The Temptations

"It's too loud!" a tiny, humpbacked lady growls as she walks past.

Quit acting like such an old lady, I think. "But it's The Temptations!" I shoot back.

"I don't think," says my buddy, Sheila, "she knows who The Temptations are."

I nod. "Maybe she thought they were a string quartet."

The rest of the crowd knows this is The Temptations. The audience might be gray, they might be bald, they might wear hearing aids, but they've come to a party like it's 1971.

Unfortunately, it is not 1971 and the years have taken their toll. Some of us struggle to our feet, clapping and singing. Then sit down and wheeze for the rest of the song. The couple next to me limps off halfway through the first set.

I lift my arms overhead, clapping and whooping to *Papa Was a Rollin' Stone.* I feel a strange sensation along my upper arms. I keep clapping and dancing as I try to pinpoint this puzzling sensation. Have I clapped so much that I've damaged the nerves in my arms? Then I stop, yanking my arms down alongside my body as Sheila twirls into the aisle.

The loose skin on my upper arms jiggles *like an old woman!* It flaps like laundry on a windy day. Thirty-five years of handstands, arm balances, headstands, and planks for nothing. Yoga has failed me.

I collapse in my seat, tucking my hands into my armpits. Maybe the couple next to me was right. Maybe I should leave, too.

Sheila beckons me up. She's laughing and dancing like she's 16 again. I pout in my seat. We are the same age, but I don't see her upper arms flapping like a sailboat in a headwind.

She turns back to smile and I see her wince. Sheila fell last week and broke two ribs. They wrapped her midsection tighter than King Tut.

I leap to my feet, belting out *My Girl* and waving my arms overhead. *Flappy arms be damned,* I think—*full speed ahead.* Next time, I'm wearing long sleeves.

Horsing Around

"We're sharing the barn with horses this weekend," Madeline tells me, rolling her eyes.

Muddy paw prints from all the agility dogs decorate my jeans. I tied my hair back to keep it out of my face, but it now looks like two squirrels have been playing dodge ball in it. I'm holding a full dog poop bag.

"The horse girls!" I clasp my hand to my mouth. "I can't face the horse girls! I look like a Munchkin rolled in horse poop."

"You kinda do," Madeline agrees.

Then a horse girl strolls past and scents the air with flowers and lavender. Long blond hair rides down her back and her tan riding pants hug a youthful booty with legs that stretch to Florida. The horse gods are very, very proud. The dog gods are very, very embarrassed.

"How do they stay so *clean*?" Madeline wonders. She looks down at what used to be shoes but are now muddy balls at the end of her legs. The horse girl's boots shine so brightly I must blink.

We smile and offer pitiful little waves, but she does not turn her head. Lesser gods and all that.

"Well, we have to be *comfortable* to run with the dogs," Kacey says as she walks past. Her hair looks like the practice ring for my squirrel dodge ball team.

"Don't they have to be *comfortable* to ride horses?" Madeline asks.

We have one side of the fairground barn, and the horses have the other. We must leash our dogs, bag their poop, and throw it in the trashcan. The barn dogs with the horse people go wherever they want and poop in our show rings. We must pick up *their* poop, bag it, and throw it in the trashcan. Again, lesser gods and all that.

I show up bright and early the next morning with clean jeans, clean sneakers and even a clean shirt. I combed my hair and scrape whatever was under my fingernails to make sure they were clean. By the time I walk to the ring, my jeans are once more covered in muddy paw prints, and I've stepped in a fresh pile of horse manure.

A horse girl strolls past, not even glancing at me. Her horse is cleaner and better groomed than a supermodel.

I hate sharing the barn with horse girls.

Scarf Shame

I look around the table and realize everyone is wearing a scarf except me. I own one scarf. A well-meaning friend gave it to me, and it hangs in my closet, mocking me. It's my favorite color, pink, and is hand embroidered. I despise it.

If I am feeling especially masochistic, I stand in front of my bathroom mirror and twist it and wind it and tuck it. Then I fling it to the floor and stomp on it.

For me, putting on a scarf is like stepping into *The Matrix*. It quickly becomes origami gone horribly wrong.

Dasha walks into yoga the next day wearing a powder blue scarf woven through her hair and a darker blue scarf draped perfectly around her neck. I force myself to compliment her and pretend to care about her trip to Mexico.

When it comes to scarves, I resemble one of those poor monkeys given a puzzle box by scheming scientists. The monkey knows there is a tasty treat inside but can't quite get the box open, delighting the scientists and causing the monkey to scream bad monkey words.

"I love scarves," Maisy says at lunch. "I can reinvent an outfit just by changing the scarf."

I grit my teeth and try to think about puppies.

They say wine helps artists create. Maybe it can help me tie a scarf. I down a glass or two of chardonnay and face the mirror once more. After five minutes, the scarf has somehow bunched itself in my fists and I'm looking for a lighter so I can set it ablaze. Luckily, I don't smoke.

I meet Barb a few days later so she can show me photos of her vacation in Scotland. Tartan fabrics and green countryside abound. We both agree our favorite thing about Scotland is the men and their accent.

"I brought you something!" Barb says, producing a thin, menacing package.

"Lovely!" I say. It contains a scarf.

"I know how much you love them!" Barb beams with pleasure.

It might be time to buy a lighter.

The List

"Who's your internist, Mom?" asks my younger son. We are discussing some routine tests with normal results.

I stare at him, mouth open. I see my internist clearly in my head, but no name comes to mind. "It begins with a W, I think."

He squints and I realize he's checking something on The List—the list my children keep to signal when it's time to send their mother *away*.

I know this because I keep a similar list for *my* mother. I've checked most of the items on her list a dozen times, but she remains firmly rooted in her condo. My brother and I even had her *tested*. She cackled with glee when she passed with flying colors.

Forgetting names of doctors, your closest friend, grandchildren, and even your sons gets you a checkmark on The List. If I remember a second or two later, I still get that look of pity and superiority. *The old bat is creeping closer to the edge*, I can hear them say. Sometimes, my older son actually says it out loud.

The picture of my doctor in my head is as clear as spring sunshine, but her name has scampered into the underbrush of my brain. Warren? Wonski? Whapshot?

I panic, I feel the gates closing behind me, locking me in a single room without even the comfort of a cat to keep me company. Not even a *cat*.

"It's okay, Mom," my younger son says. He shakes his head at the old woman who is ready for not-quite-so-active retirement living. I picture a place named *Sleeping Peacefully* or *She Had a Good Run But You Can't Live by Yourself Forever*.

In my children's heads, I'm already drooling in my oatmeal.

My son turns toward the door.

"Wilson!" I shout. "Her name is Wilson!"

I cackle with glee.

Tooth Ache

"I think," says my vet, "you should take Pip to the doggie dentist."

"No," I moan. "Not the doggie dentist! *Anything* but the doggie dentist!"

Nothing strikes fear in a dog owner's heart more than the words *doggie dentist*. We all know what happens there—unspeakable torture. Unspeakable torture of the financial kind. I've seen grown men weep when handed the bill from the doggie dentist.

I've wept when handed the bill from the doggie dentist. Dog owners shamed into visiting the doggie dentist fill the poorhouse.

"Couldn't you just *pull* the teeth?"

The vet looks at me as if I were Ebenezer Scrooge chastising Tiny Tim. "He's a young dog. We should try to save his teeth."

"Well, he's not *that* young."

"Just give me a good pair of pliers and I'll yank them out!" my dad used to say when faced with a dental bill. I now know exactly how he felt.

"You don't want him to end up like Scout," the vet reminds me. Scout, my cattle dog, has zip, zero, zilch teeth. A genetic disorder laid waste to her mouth. Pip has two broken teeth. Even if they pull those, he'll still be 40 ahead of Scout. Besides, Scout has no teeth and seems to manage just fine. I mean, really, how many teeth does a pampered pet need?

I go to the dentist. She opens Pip's mouth and examines the damage. "You give him too many bones."

I nod my head in shame. Atonement, I realize, is going to cost me—big time.

"We can save one, but the other has too much damage." She will do a root canal on the one tooth. Luckily, she says, it doesn't need a cap. She shows me an example of a shiny metal cap they place on some dogs. It could be worse, I realize, Pip could have ended up with a *grill*. Of course, if Pip had a grill, he would have a diamond or two in it.

The dentist leaves the room, and an assistant walks in carrying the estimate. She hands me a piece of paper with several large numbers on it. My checkbook begins to wail.

I sign the estimate and they lead Pip to the operating room. Later that afternoon, I come to pick him up. They show me the bill and I try not to sob as I hand over my credit card. They lead out a groggy Pip who snuggles into my arms.

"It's a good thing you're cute," I say as I carry him to the car.

Next time, just give me a good pair of pliers.

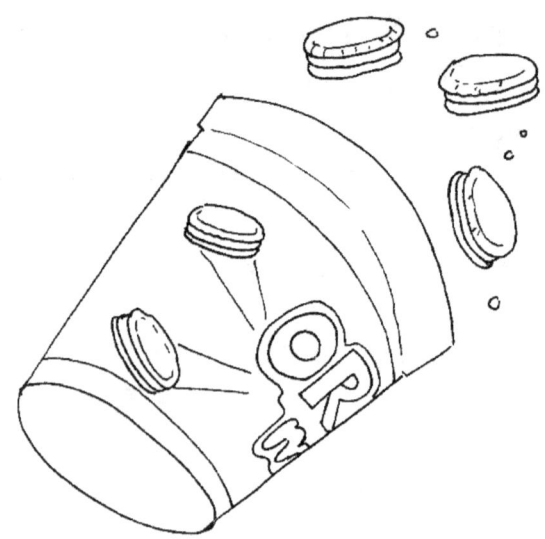

Nana the Narc

My granddaughter and grandson are fighting over the iPad. The whining, I know, will soon turn to screaming. I am wedged in the back seat of the minivan, looking out the window and pretending I see a peaceful meadow surrounded by springtime flowers.

My daughter-in-law tries to mediate the escalating war before shoes, toys, and even Nana's purse become weaponized. I try to envision puppies and kittens in my meadow.

"She started it!" my grandson fires. I flinch just a bit.

"It's *his* fault!" my granddaughter retorts. She slams her fists on the arms of her car seat.

I know we have another 45 minutes on this journey. I begin to mumble, *Serenity now.*

"Actually, *he* started it," I say before I can stop myself. Nanas are kind. Nanas are fun. Nanas are *not* narcs.

Both grandkids whip their head around to glare at me. I smile uneasily. I have just thrust myself into the middle of Thunderdome. Karma is not kind to the stupid.

My daughter-in-law negotiates a truce. We all sit staring out the window. My meadow has morphed into a decaying battlefield littered with broken promises and obsolete weapons. *Bad Nana*, I tell myself.

"Snack!" the baby cries. They entrusted me with a backpack full of food. As I open it, I spy a package of Oreos, my favorite treat in the entire universe. I quickly stash it in my pocket.

I pass out granola bars and juice boxes and the truce seems to hold.

"Cookies!" the baby cries. "You promise!"

"I know I packed some," my daughter-in-law puzzles. "Can you look again?"

I mumble a reply, my mouth full of Oreos. I try to look like I've never heard the word "cookie" before.

"Nana ate them!" my grandson crows. I bow my head. Karma, indeed, is not kind to the stupid.

Are You Going to the Renaissance Fair?

"Huzzah!" my son shouts as he walks in my front door. "I have tickets to the Renaissance Fair!"

"That's nice," I reply, trailing after my grandson as he prepares to deconstruct my kitchen.

"I got a ticket for you, too, Mom," my son adds. "You want to go, don't you?" He gives me puppy dog eyes. "There's wine."

"I'd love to go." I remind myself that any time spent with my son and his family is my favorite time. Even if there are costumes involved.

That weekend, we pack up the car and drive 90 minutes through the springtime desert. The baby naps the entire way and I enjoy the orange, blue and bright pink flowers lining the road. I imagine we will spend an hour or so strolling the grounds and then head home. I will be back in time for a nap.

We see massive clouds of dust before we see the parking lot. Instead of noble steeds, hundreds of cars line up as knights, princesses, pirates, fairies, and even a Jedi or two head for the entrance. I feel seriously underdressed.

If you're ever feeling nostalgic for the 1960s and/or hippies, just hop on over to your local Renaissance Fair. Think Woodstock in King Arthur's court.

I am strolling with my son, daughter-in-law, and the baby past booths featuring fairies, mermaids, swords, tapestries, dragons, and even codpieces. Yes, an entire booth devoted to codpieces. I sneak in several long stares before we move on.

I taste mead for the first time. How have I not discovered this before? Wine made from honey!

I admire the young knights and envy the pretty maids. Several women my age trot past wearing fairy costumes. I try to picture myself dressed in similar garb and shudder. Small children would shriek and run to their mothers if I attempted any type of Tinkerbell in public.

My grandson laughs on the rides, we eat turkey legs, we watch hawks perform tricks, we stroll for hours and never see the same thing twice. As the sun slides west, we pack up and head for the car, exhausted in a delicious kind of way.

"Want to go again next year?" my son asks as he pulls out of the parking lot.

"Huzzah!" I shout.

Vegas Blues

We slide into choice seats at the crowded bar. We are in the lobby of the Aria Hotel in Vegas and it's Saturday night. Our basketball team has just won the conference championship and we're ready to party.

Waiters place pretty drinks in front of folks on either side of us. I catch the bartender's eye, but he shakes his head and looks away.

We are ladies of a certain age floating in a sea of youth.

"They're not going to serve us," Carolyn shouts. "They don't want us at the bar." It's true, servers don't even look at us. We are invisible. Or maybe way too visible.

It hits me like a sledgehammer—I am too old to get a drink at a bar in Vegas. I look at my companions. We are more or less fashionably dressed, we obviously have a little money, and we're thirsty.

But we are too old. To be served a drink. In the Aria Hotel. In Las Vegas.

Just shoot me now.

I *really, really* need a drink.

Too thirsty to argue, we slink off our seats and head to another bar. The beautiful young woman at the podium tells us they are full. Empty tables abound.

"I know the kind of place you're looking for," she stage whispers. "You want someplace with food, too."

Actually, we do. For a moment, I fear she will direct us to a Denny's.

She points toward a Mexican food place tucked into a corner. With almost no lighting, it is the perfect place to hide our ancient faces. We accept defeat and find a table.

No server comes. For eons. I am so hungry and thirsty now that I am tempted to find a Denny's. Besides, it is *way* past my bedtime.

"Do we have plague sores sprouting from our noses?" asks my buddy, Diane. We check each other carefully.

"There you are!" shouts Trish. "I've been looking all over for you guys!" Trish is in her early 40s and has the kind of dark beauty that makes everyone stare.

She plops down and immediately begins dissecting the basketball game. Suddenly, a server appears with a bowl of chips and glasses of water. We pounce like wolves on a fresh carcass.

"I thought you guys would be in the bar," Trish says.

So did we, Trish, so did we.

The Big Bag of Dog Food

"In the long term, of course, the stock market always goes up." I am sitting in my financial advisor's office, trying to sound like I know what I'm talking about.

"True," she says, leaning across her desk toward me. "But in your case, we aren't thinking *too* long term."

I remember taking my 15-year-old dog to the vet years ago. He examined her and shook his head. "I wouldn't buy the big bag of dog food if I were you," he said.

My financial advisor is telling me not to buy the big bag of dog food when it comes to stocks. Or toilet paper. Or paper towels. Or anything else.

I look to see if she is kidding, but she is serious. My financial welfare is her only concern, she says.

Obviously, she doesn't give a hoot about my psychological welfare.

My next stop is lunch with friends. As I wait for a table to be cleared, I notice a mother and her teenage son sitting on a bench. She nudges him up. She smiles, indicating the spot next to her.

I turn around to see who she is beckoning and realize it is *me*. I am the old woman who is too feeble to stand. This day just gets better and better.

I tell her my table will be ready in a minute and thank her. What I don't tell her is that it is easier to just stand. If I sit, I will have to get back up again on arthritic hips and knees.

My friends soon join me at a table. "I don't have a Costco membership," Anna says as she spears a piece of cucumber. "I don't know what I would buy there."

"Wine," Beth and I say at the same time.

Costco just happens to be next on my list and I stroll the aisles looking for samples and good deals. I glance at a double box of cereal but pass it by, remembering my financial advisor's words.

I find myself in the wine aisle and pick up a couple of bottles. Then I remember my financial advisor. And the nice lady who wanted me to sit down. Maybe I shouldn't buy the *big* bag of cereal, but I turn back to the wine aisle. I *will* buy the big case of wine. And maybe some chocolate.

I Fly Over the Cuckoo's Nest

"You can't sit around all summer," my father informs me. "I've found you a volunteer position at the state mental hospital."

"A mental hospital?" I am 14 years old and imagined I would sit around watching TV and talking on the phone like any girl my age. I feel I have the *right* to fritter my summer away discussing boys and hairstyles—and watching *The Monkees* on television.

My father is a social worker and hospital administrator. "We must all be useful," is his mantra.

I have seen the movies—mental hospitals are where they lock up killers who will sneak up and murder you with a shiv made from a plastic spoon. Or worse.

"I don't want to!" I protest.

"And yet you will."

He drives me to my first morning and drops me off with a slightly fuzzy older woman who seems confused about why I'm here. I'm not entirely sure she is an employee. She seems like someone the inmates would keep as a hostage when they negotiate.

Madge, the possible employee/inmate, leads me to an arts and crafts room. Several older women paint and play with construction paper. They smile and go back to their work.

Madge sits behind a glass wall reading a magazine and smoking a cigarette. I walk around the room praising the women for their drawings of stick figures and houses.

Madge doesn't look up from her magazine when someone knocks on the door. Like the fool that I am, I flip the lock and open it. An older gentleman stands there, smiling. I am knocked backwards by the sudden stench and clasp my hand over my mouth.

I hear Madge drop her magazine and walk briskly toward us.

"Go back to your room, Mr. Basil," Madge orders. "Right now."

Mr. Basil reaches into his front shirt pocket, extracting what I think is a Tootsie Roll. He offers it to me. Some primal part of my brain makes me back away.

It takes another second or two before I realize the brown thing in his hand is definitely *not* a Tootsie Roll. He has smeared some on his cheek.

Madge slams the door. She turns to smile at me. "Let's send you down to admissions. You can help them with filing."

Betting on the Turtle

"Look what the Browns gave us!" my boys declared 30 years ago, jumping up and down for joy. Inside a massive aquarium sat a water turtle aptly named Myrtle.

The Browns were famous for acquiring exotic pets and then losing interest. A few years before, they "gave" my boys a veiled chameleon. The boys, of course, soon lost interest. I spent every morning dangling live mealworms in its face until it died at the ripe, old age of four.

Myrtle proved more tenacious than the chameleon and has survived for 30 years. She used to eat anything I dropped in her aquarium—small fish, crayfish, and especially snails. She loved the way they crunched and would literally jump for joy as they slid into the water.

Then one day, a goldfish survived Myrtle's jaws. I came in the next morning to find it swimming amidst the rocks. The fish was still there the next day and the next. How sweet, I thought, Myrtle has a friend.

Months went by. I made the mistake of naming the goldfish. I called her Goldie and fed her every morning when I fed Myrtle. Goldie doubled her size and Myrtle ignored her.

Then one morning, I walked in to find Goldie floating belly up with Myrtle-sized chunks missing from her body. It turns out, Myrtle was just fattening her up. She is the Hannibal Lector of turtles.

But these days, Goldie could swim fearlessly, were she still alive. Myrtle and I have grown old together. I have fed her for 30 years. The family who owned her before me had her for five.

Neither boy volunteered to take her when they moved out on their own. Now Myrtle and I compete to see who will last the longest. I'm betting on the turtle.

When she quit eating live food, I took her to the turtle vet. "Try canned dog food," he said. It worked for five years and then once more, she refused to eat. This time, the turtle vet x-rayed her, probed her, and took blood samples.

"We know she's at least 35 years old." He shook his head. "They usually only live 40 to 50 years. We have no idea how old she really is." I cried, clutching Myrtle to my chest.

I cried even more when they handed me a bill for $400.

I thanked the vet, packed up Myrtle and began to trudge out of the office. "You know," the vet called after me. "You might try a nice piece of salmon."

It turns out, Myrtle loves salmon. Can't get enough of it.

Like I said, I'm betting on the turtle.

Jeopardy!

"Macedonia," I half whisper. "What is Macedonia?"

Ken Jennings finishes reading the clue.

"What is Northern Greece?" says the middle contestant.

"Macedonia!" I shout. "What is Macedonia?"

"The answer is Macedonia," Ken informs him.

I am surrounded by idiots.

A commercial appears and I fast forward. I always record *Jeopardy!* so I don't have to watch the commercials. Especially all the drug ads for conditions I didn't even know existed. By the end of the ad, I'm convinced I now have the previously unknown malady.

Other than Macedonia, this batch of contestants seems to know what they're doing. The buzzers ring and the answers fly, and everyone is winning money.

"Who is Henry VIII?" the returning champion says.

"Henry VIII?!" I stand up, shaking my fist at the TV. "It was Richard III! Everyone knows it's Richard III!!" Babes in arms know it was Richard III, for heaven's sake! Where do they get these people!?

Another commercial appears and I collapse back on the couch, fast forwarding through ads for ambulance chasing attorneys. I linger over a spot with a particularly handsome fellow. If I get in an accident, I'm calling him.

Now the three contestants appear on the screen. Ken (We are on a first name basis, I feel.) walks up to the contestants, preparing to find out about their fascinating lives.

I press fast forward again. I'm not interested in their lives. Those folks are such *nerds*.

The Kraken

"You HATE me!" my beloved granddaughter yells as she slams her fists on the restaurant table. I look around, afraid someone will call the cops and the headline will read, "Worst Nana *Ever* Locked Up for the Rest of Her Life."

I don't know how this all began. We were at the zoo, and we decided to go to lunch. Then my granddaughter melted into a puddle of tears and snot and screams. She looks like one of the witches from *Macbeth* who has been eating eye of newt just a little *too* long.

I have no sisters and only raised sons, so little girls are a bit of a mystery to me. Make that a *terrifying* mystery to me.

I offer her strawberry lemonade. A cookie. I try singing a song, but she flashes me a look that makes me practically wet my pants.

I have released the Kraken and I have no idea how to get it back in its cave.

She is six years old. Now I know why some folks sent their girls off to be nuns. Let God figure them out.

If she is like this at six, I will need to build a bomb shelter before she hits thirteen.

Then she calls me a name. A name little girls shouldn't be able to pronounce.

"You do *not* call your Nana names!" I'm sure now I face imprisonment without any judge or jury. I snapped at my granddaughter and deserve whatever punishment they dish out.

I drop my head, waiting for the Grandmother Police to grab me and cart me away.

Then something brushes against me and climbs onto my lap. She rests her head against my chest, and I try to wipe the hair out of her eyes. The tears and snot glue it firmly into place.

"Everything okay?" the server asks.

"Nanas make everything better," my granddaughter says, smiling at the server.

I don't know what the heck just happened, but the Kraken seems to have retreated to its cave.

I just hope it stays there.

Rise of the Zombies

The zombies are rising in my backyard. It looks like *Day of the Dead*. And I'm pretty sure they are coming for *me*.

It's my fault they are entombed. I'm the one who bought them and delivered them to that instrument of evil, the dread zombie creator herself, my cattle dog, Scout.

Now these furry creatures taunt me with a fuzzy paw in that corner and a protruding ear next to the wall. The rain last night freed them from their earthly graves, exposing them to the brilliant morning light.

They are staring at me. I just know it. They seek revenge.

Once, they were happy furry chew toys carried around the house and yard in all their plush glory. Now they rot in the ground. When I try to pull them up, roots cling to their dirty skin.

I tried washing to restore their lively colors, their soft fur. They disintegrated in the washer, pieces of flotsam and jetsam stuck to the washer's tub. It was like a battlefield scene—a fuzzy Armageddon.

"I'm sorry," I whisper as I survey the carnage. "I didn't know this would happen."

That's a lie. I knew perfectly well that Scout buries her toys. She'll be proudly carrying her new bunny or squirrel, or hedgehog and I'll think, she loves this one—this one she'll let live.

But she doesn't. No matter how cuddly, how soft, how adorable, they end up as zombie toys, rotting in the backyard, awaiting the next desert rain to free them. But they are never free—they have become one of the living dead.

And I brought them to this fate. They dream of rising and smothering me in dirt and rocks and roots.

Luckily for me, they are stuffed toys that will continue to molder in the ground.

At least, I hope so.

Hear Me Roar!

"Easily assembled with only a Phillips screwdriver," the ad says. The website shows a darling child-sized table and two chairs perfect for coloring, building and snacking.

The last thing I remember assembling was a sandwich, so I hesitate. Wait a minute, I can do this! I am an educated woman. I know which one is the Phillips screwdriver. I am woman—hear me roar!

When the package arrives, I know immediately—I am woman—watch me cry.

I grab a box cutter and start slashing at the cardboard container. As far as I can tell it is *only* packaging. I slash, I rip, I say bad words. Finally, I strike a piece of wood. Of course, it's wrapped in more packaging.

So far, I need a box cutter and a screwdriver. Although at this point, I am considering pouring the kind of screwdriver, that contains alcohol.

I finally unearth the instructions. As I fish them out of the box, each page flutters in a different direction. I say a few more bad words.

After 45 minutes of unwrapping, I have enough packaging to clog the Pacific Ocean. So now I need a box cutter, a screwdriver and access to a landfill.

I manage to assemble the little table. I am so proud that I take a photo and send it to my sons. They don't believe me.

No matter how hard I try, the seat of the chair refuses to wed the legs. More bad words ensue. My daughter-in-law, the engineer, generously comes over and takes a look. She unscrews pieces, she bangs, she says even more bad words. Somehow, she makes it fit.

So, now to assemble the table and chairs, I need a box cutter, a screwdriver, and access to a landfill, and an engineer. I add wine to my list. Now I won't *care* if the pieces fit.

After three days and a festival of bad words, the pieces all come together. I have three screws leftover. I throw them in the trash before anyone notices.

My grandson races in the door, stops and stares for a second at the little table and chairs, and then gently sits. "Mine," he says.

I am woman—hear me roar!

Dead Woman Walking

"Will you still be alive in June?" Carmen's granddaughter asked recently.

"I told her I would be back in June for her dance recital," Carmen says at lunch. "She thinks I'm about to die!"

Carmen does Pilates twice a week and walks every day. She eats reasonably well and maintains a healthy weight, but this child doubts her ability to survive even a few more months.

I nod my head in sympathy.

"Are you really, really, really old?" my grandson asks a few days later.

I ponder for a second. "Only one *really*," I tell him.

He gives me a skeptical look. I can tell he thinks I am at least three *reallys*—maybe even four or five.

My son recently informed me that he hated being left with his grandparents when he was a child. He worried they would die while he was in their care. They were *my* age.

I thought my grandmothers were ancient when I was a child. They were *my* age.

"How old are you?" my granddaughter asks on a regular basis. When I tell her, she gets wide-eyed and gives me a big hug.

She thinks I am about to kick the bucket, shove off, die, expire. To her, I am a dead woman walking.

To keep the ravages of time at bay, I try to at least dress in a trendy fashion. But my sagging chin, my wiggly arm fat, and my swollen knuckles are the truth tellers. I'm just putting lipstick on a pig when I buy the latest fashion trend.

But at least it's the *latest* shade of lipstick on a dead woman walking.

Protest Music

"It's a play built around Bob Dylan music," Darcy, one of our group leaders, explains. That should have been my first clue. Bob Dylan is not famous for songs about holding hands and capering through fields of rainbows.

"*Girl from the North Country* is set during the Depression," she adds over her shoulder as she leads us out of the hotel. *There's the second clue*, I now realize.

My third clue should have been that Dan, our fearless leader, opted to see a *different* play that night, leaving Darcy to shepherd 15 women of a certain age onto a New York subway and into the theater. A flock of parakeets in the wilds of Borneo would be easier to herd than this group. We stop and stare at people and buildings, tripping over curbs and each other.

We saw *My Fair Lady* at Lincoln Center the night before, so our heads are full of graceful lyrics and gorgeous costumes. I hum *I Could Have Danced All Night* as Darcy grabs my arm, propelling me onto the subway car.

After losing only one group member in the theater, we settle in our seats at The Public Theater. The entry door should have a sign saying, "Abandon hope, all ye who enter here".

Gracious, efficient ushers discovered our missing woman who froze when confronted with bathroom signs telling her to choose whatever restroom makes her feel most comfortable. "What do they mean by *comfortable*?" she whispers to me as the music begins.

Dylan is famous for his songs of protest and longing. Within a few minutes, I wanted to protest the subject and longed to find the exit. The acting and singing were beautiful, the sets clever, the dialog sharp and crisp. One character has dementia, another is a fake minister, alcoholics abound, a father drowns a son—the fun never stops.

The lights go up and we stand, looking like pedestrians who have just witnessed a 40-car pileup.

"Well," says Kathy, "it did give me a new appreciation of Dylan's music."

"I suppose," says another woman, moving like a sleepwalker.

"I don't know about you gals," says Alice, "but I could use a scotch."

"I don't drink scotch," I say, "but I might make an exception this time."

We stampede toward the bar.

Shoe Business

A Nordstrom shoe sale! I click *quit* on my work file and switch to more important matters—shopping!

Row after row of sensible sandals and oxfords scrolls across my computer screen. Where are the cute ones? The strappy sandals? The glittered sneakers?

My blood runs cold. I remember what my media-savvy son recently told me. Nordstrom's computers are showing me what they think I will buy. They think I am an old woman who wears oxfords and orthopedic sandals.

Son of a biscuit!

I admit I occasionally buy sensible shoes, but only when I need them for travel or playing with the grandkids. Most of my shoes are cute and sometimes even sassy in a *look-my-feet-are-still-in-their-forties* kind of way.

I gave up four-inch heels decades ago, but that doesn't mean Mama has to abandon looking *good*.

I click back to my email screen, disgusted for the moment with computers. I notice emails for walk-in tubs, funeral services, and creams for aging skin.

To quote Monty Python, "I am not dead yet." But Big Brother is pretty sure I'm on my way to corpse city— and I'm getting there in sensible shoes.

Furious now, I scroll down to high heels and trendsetters. I will prove this computer wrong!

Hmmmm. Orange shoes? No way—my feet would look like lifeboats. Fuzzy slipper shoes? The first drop of rain would ruin them. Shoes with straps that wrap up my legs? Aging Hooker is not a look I am currently cultivating.

I scroll back up, just a little. There! A pair of leopard skin pumps with two-inch heels. Sassy, and maybe just a tad sensible.

I click *buy* and feel vindicated. Just to show Nordstrom, I think I will splurge on another pair— maybe those cute silver sandals. I'm going to teach this store a lesson!

Then an ad pops up for a pair of black sandals with a padded sole and elastic straps. Those would be comfy, I reason. I could wear them to the grocery store or on outings with the grandkids. And they would be perfect for travel!

Maybe Nordstrom knows me better than I thought.

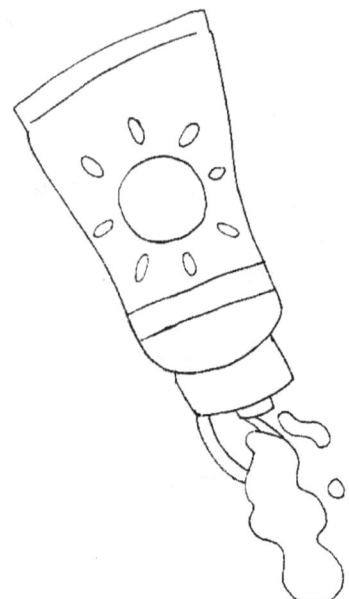

Tan Lines

I lounged for hours in the Arizona sun as a teenager. Wrinkles and cancer were never my concern. I wanted to look *good* with tan legs that would attract boys.

It worked. My ex-husband said he first noticed my legs.

When my blond boys were born, I converted to a sunscreen fanatic. My boys never left the house without sunscreen on those lily-white arms, legs, and faces. "You'll thank me when you're 80," I used to say when they accused me of being a sunscreen Nazi.

Like all Nazis, I am a hypocrite. I secretly refused to put sunscreen on my legs, hoping for that perfect shade of brown. I wore a bathing suit while I did yard work and wore shorts *long* after anyone wanted to see my legs, tan or white.

My son suggests a trip to the Arizona-Sonora Desert Museum on a spring day. I grab my hat, my sunglasses, and my shorts. After all, at this age, what harm could a little sun do? If sun damage takes 20 years to materialize, my skin won't wrinkle until I'm drooling in my oatmeal.

Four hours later, I peel off my shorts expecting to see the perfect tan. The reflection from my alabaster skin almost blinds me. My legs, with their white skin and varicose veins, resemble an ancient map of the tributaries of the Amazon.

My legs, unprotected for hours in the desert sun, refuse to turn even one skin cell the slightest shade of brown. They are whiter than an albino polar bear.

Are my tanning cells already dead? Is this Mother Nature's way of saying, "Wear pants for heaven's sake!"

Mother Nature always has the last laugh, but I'm not ready to let her win just yet.

If Mother Nature won't help me, I'm just going to help myself. I buy a massive tube of self-tanning cream. I still want to look *good*.

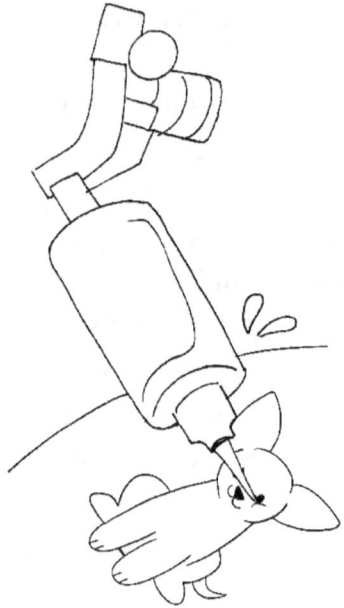

Tattoo Temptation

"I'm thinking of getting a tattoo," my friend, Anna, says as she sips her white wine. We're solving the world's problems this evening over happy hour.

I raise one eyebrow and dig into the salsa with a delightfully salty chip.

"Just a little one," she says. "Someplace where no one would see it."

In my case, I think, that would be just about *any* place. It's been a long time since my last date.

"Something about my kids, maybe," Anna adds.

"That is just what every child wants—to be memorialized on their mother's backside," I remind her.

"I worry, though, about the blood," she says.

"You mean there's *blood* when you get a tattoo?" I almost spit out my wine.

"Of course," Anna tells me. "They pierce your skin with a needle and inject the ink under the skin." She picks up a chip and studies it. "They use paper towels to mop it up as they go along."

"Man, they don't *make* enough wine for me to do that," I say.

"You're not supposed to be drunk," Anna chides me. "It makes you bleed more."

Silly me—I always thought being drunk was necessary for getting a tattoo.

"Besides, it's not respectful to the artist to be drunk," she adds.

Personally, I'm wondering just how respectful it is to ask the artist to memorialize your pet Chihuahua on your butt.

"And there's the pain," she says. "My girlfriend almost fainted when she got hers."

"This idea sounds better and better," I tell her.

"And you sit still for a long time. When Jenny got hers, she laid on her side for three hours."

"Tell me again why you're thinking of getting a tattoo."

"I thought it would be fun." Anna lifts her glass of wine, and we toast.

"To definitely *not* getting a tattoo," I declare as our glasses clink.

Cashing Out

I don't have time to run into the grocery store. But I'm out of blueberries, cereal and some other items that may, or may not, include a bottle of wine.

The lines at the checkout counters snake through the store. I dash to the self-serve machines, the ones I almost always avoid. Machines sense that I'm vulnerable and an idiot.

Check-out clerks take one look and know I'm going to need help. Machines can't wait to remind me of my human frailty.

I square my shoulders. I am a modern woman. I can do this.

Turns out, I can't.

I scan my first item and place it in the bag.

"Please place the item in the bag," the machine says.

"I did," I shoot back.

"Please place the item in the bag," she repeats, a little more forcefully now.

I pick up the box of cereal and show it to her. "It's *in* the bag."

The supervising clerk steps closer. "Can I help you?"

"I put it in the bag!" Ha! I tattled to the clerk—now the machine will get what's coming to it.

The clerk looks at the computer screen, then eyes me up and down, no doubt calculating if it's time to call security. She flashes a badge at the screen and the voice quiets.

I ask the clerk about her day, but she turns to another machine that is sassing a customer. Perhaps the machines choose this moment to rise.

I scan the next few items and the machine is quietly contrite. My mistake is feeling cocky. Machines can't stand it if you're cocky.

"Please scan the item," the machine instructs me.

"I did!" I hold the blueberries up to the screen and shake them. "See?"

"Please scan the item."

I'm really going to need that bottle of wine.

The Wave

"Well, this year," my eye doctor says, "might be the year you need cataract surgery. I don't want you wrapping your car around a tree."

"It's definitely arthritis," my orthopedic surgeon says the next day. "You know, you're not 40 anymore."

Thanks for the update, Captain Obvious.

My next stop is the dental hygienist, an impossibly perky gal who always makes me smile.

I tell her about the cataract surgery. "I've always wanted cataract surgery," she chirps, "then I won't need to wear glasses."

I tell her about the arthritis. "Most of my patients are way younger than you when they develop it."

"Lie to me," I tell her. "Don't say anything about my aging mouth."

She pokes around my teeth with a frightfully sharp object. She reports numbers to her assistant, who records them. "3, 2, 942, 219," she calls.

She whips the frightfully sharp object out of my mouth. "No blood!" she tells the assistant.

"She hardly ever says *that*!" the assistant reports, beaming at me.

"You have a very young mouth!" my hygienist declares. She turns to her assistant. "Let's do The Wave." They do an abbreviated version of The Wave seen in stadiums. I blush.

As I prepare to leave, she turns to get my complimentary toothbrush and floss. She digs in a drawer, then smiles. She peels off a gold star and places it ceremoniously on my shirt.

I practically skip out of the office. I feel like a kid again.

Yoga with Yoda

"Hello, my beauties," Lottie, my yoga teacher, says as she walks into the room.

Lottie settles on her mat, facing two rows of students. "Do you have any yoga questions?"

I've taken Lottie's classes for years. Unfortunately, this means she knows what I can and cannot do—like Master Yoda training Jedis.

Those of us who are in the trenches sit together, avoiding eye contact. *Don't say anything. Don't say anything*, we silently plead.

"Actually," pipes up a new student. "My hips and lower back are a little tight." Like Luke Skywalker facing Yoda for the first time, she is not afraid. She will be. She will be.

"Excellent!" Lottie declares. I whimper like the coward I am.

Puddles of sweat drip on my mat as I struggle through hip opener after hip opener. I will be lucky if I can crawl out of bed in the morning.

Her regular students know where Lottie is going. We tremble like the rebels watching Darth Vader approaching. Sure enough, she demonstrates The Handstand.

"I'm not sure how The Handstand is a hip opener," the new student says. Young Skywalker has much to learn.

I know there will come a time when The Handstand is beyond my abilities, and I can plead the weakness of aging. Today is not that day. Lottie is not having it.

"Give it a try," Lottie commands. In Lottie language, that means, get up or go home. We get up.

As I thud back to my mat, I glance over at the new student, who is curled in a ball.

Lottie puts her arm around Young Skywalker, whispering words of encouragement. She helps her legs up on the wall and holds her for a second or two.

The student drops down, smiling.

We regulars look at each other and nod. We are always happy to welcome a new Jedi in training.

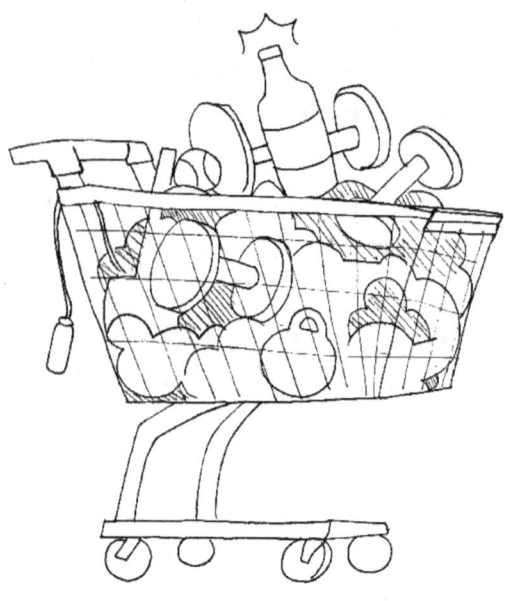

Wine Not?

I stand in the wine section at Costco, pondering what might taste good. It is summer, so I lean toward a case of reasonably priced chardonnay. One brand has a screw top. *Yes, folks, it's a winner!*

I step forward to lift the case into my cart. (Before you judge me, this will last a long time. Well, at least a decent amount of time. OK, a reasonably long time. Oh, heck, it will last as long as it lasts.)

I scoop up the case, but it refuses to budge.

I bend my knees, take a deep breath, and give it the old heave ho. Nothing. Nada. The case has grown roots to the center of the earth.

Perhaps, I think, *this case is somehow stuck.* That's it. Someone has accidentally glued these cases together.

I step to the next case. After several embarrassing grunts and a lot of sweat, it remains in place.

I glance around—here comes a lady from church, smiling and waving. *Son of a biscuit!*

"You must be having a party," she says as I clutch my case of screw top chardonnay.

"Book club," I lie.

"Oh, yes, I've heard a lot of drinking goes on at book club," she says.

"You have no idea."

She helps me hoist the case into my cart. We chat and then she wanders down the liquor aisle. Hmmmm—maybe she has book club, too.

As I head toward the checkout line, I pause. How am I going to get this case into my car? Am I now reduced to buying six bottles at a time? In a few more years, will it be three at a time? If that happens, I might as well just camp in the Costco parking lot.

I spot the solution. There, next to tennis balls and skateboards, is a set of weights.

"Going to start working out?" the clerk says as he scans my purchases.

"I thought I'd give it a try," I admit. "Gotta stay in shape."

In shape for wine, that is.

Grandson Blues

"So," says Grandson Number 2, "how was your day, Nana?"

Grandson 2 is seven years old and calls on his parents' phones. His mother, I know, is having a girls' night out.

"I tried to call Mom first, but she didn't answer," Grandson 2 says, "so I called you, Nana." For once in my life, I don't mind playing second fiddle—he called me!

"Quit playing with Dad's guitar. If that string snaps, it will put your eye out!" Grandson Number 1 (who is 14) warns. "I want to talk to Nana!"

"I'm just playing it!" Grandson 2 shouts.

"What if you break two strings? You could go blind in both eyes! Is that what you want?"

"Where's your dad?" I say.

"He's cleaning the pool," Grandson 1 says. "Dad's going to be mad if you break his guitar. That's his good one!"

"What are you doing, Nana?" Grandson 2 ignores his older brother, which is like throwing dry brush on a campfire.

"I want to talk to Nana!" I hear a bit of scuffling. "Quit trying to staple yourself!" Grandson 1 yells.

"Maybe you two should step out of your dad's office," I suggest. More scuffling noises ensue.

"Go watch *Bluey*!" the older one yells.

"So, Nana," Grandson 2 continues, "look at this chain. I'll explain it later. It is a funny story."

"She's not on Facetime! She can't see you!"

"Can you see me, Nana?"

I explain I cannot. Grandson 2 launches into a story of how he acquired a new Lego. It is a long story. I nod and try to imagine what Grandson 1 is doing. It's like knowing there is a shark swimming close by in murky water.

The TV blares. It is the cartoon show *Bluey*. All my grandchildren love *Bluey*, but Grandson 2 tells me the plot of every episode when I visit.

"Hey," shouts Grandson 1, "*Bluey* is on!"

"Bye, Nana!" yells Grandson 2.

"So," says Grandson 1, "how was your day, Nana?"

Going to the Dogs

"You know," says my friend, Eileen, scanning my bedroom, "this is actually the *dogs'* bedroom. They just let you sleep here."

I look around at three dog beds, two crates, and a blanket-covered chair.

My bedroom has, literally, gone to the dogs. And I only have *two* dogs.

I never intended this to happen. First were the crates, where the pups slept until they were potty trained. I wash their blankets every week, but otherwise I'm not allowed to touch them.

Then Scout needed her *own* bed because arthritis sometimes impinges on her ability to climb on *my* bed.

Then, because Scout had *her* own bed, Pip wanted *his* bed. It's only fair.

The third dog bed is for when the other two simply won't *do*.

Then I bought a soft, cuddly blanket for what used to be my reading chair. The dogs requisitioned it as their lookout post. I'm not even allowed to sit in it at night.

The bedspread, of course, retired years ago. It was a little scratchy for their delicate hides.

They allow me a slice of the human bed. If I don't toss and turn *too* much, I can stay. But I can't use Pip's pillow. There are limits to his largesse.

Eileen doesn't understand. She has *cats*.

"Darling, you *must* take back your bedroom," she insists. As a decorator, she has all kinds of ideas—pillows, delicate throws, airy fabrics. I don't have the heart to say what the pups will do to her lovely ideas. Body fluids and flying hair would certainly be involved.

We talk colors and paint and moving furniture. As we walk to the front door, she places her hand gently on my arm. "You can do this. It can be *your* bedroom again."

It's never been my bedroom. I'm just grateful the dogs let me sleep there.

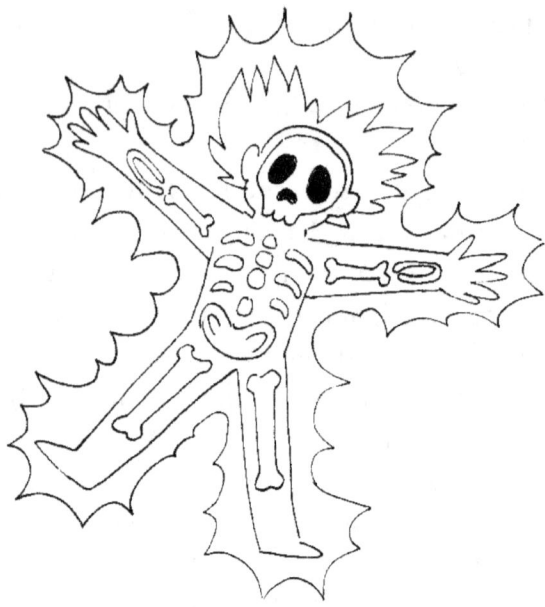

Shock Wave

"Ever been shocked before?" the handsome doctor asks me.

When my husband of 42 years walked out the door, I think.

"I grabbed an electric fence once," I say.

"This won't be nearly as bad," he says. *Darn*, he's wearing a wedding ring.

I'm having some kind of nerve conduction test. My orthopedist suggested I enroll in a study of a new arthritis medication. To be considered, I must undergo a marathon of medical tests. I gave multiple syringes of blood, peed more often in a jar than the toilet, and had *two* MRIs. A battalion of medical professionals has poked and prodded me (and not in a good way).

This, they assure me, is the last test.

The doctor places little pads along my leg and foot. "Here we go," he says. A tingle makes the muscle in my foot twitch.

The doctor looks at the monitor. "We need a 2.0 for this study. Your reading is 1.9." He fiddles with some dials. "This should do it."

My entire foot jumps as I stifle a yelp.

"Hmmm," the doctor says. He fiddles again with the dials. "There's nothing wrong with your nerves," he assures me. "You have a small muscle."

"Let's try it again." He smiles. I begin to sweat.

"Yikes!" My leg does an Irish jig. I look down to make sure it isn't smoking. I desperately hope I haven't soiled myself.

"There we go," he says. He smiles and walks out the door. I curl into a ball and whimper.

The nice lady who supervises the study comes to get me. "You've passed all the tests!"

But I'm not sure I'll ever walk again. I roll off the exam table and grab hold of a handy chair.

"I'll call you tomorrow." She smiles as if I've just won a marathon.

I hobble to my car. I decide it's never too early for vodka.

She calls the next day. "I'm so sorry," she says, "but there are too many people in the study. It turns out, we can't use you."

Now *that* is shocking.

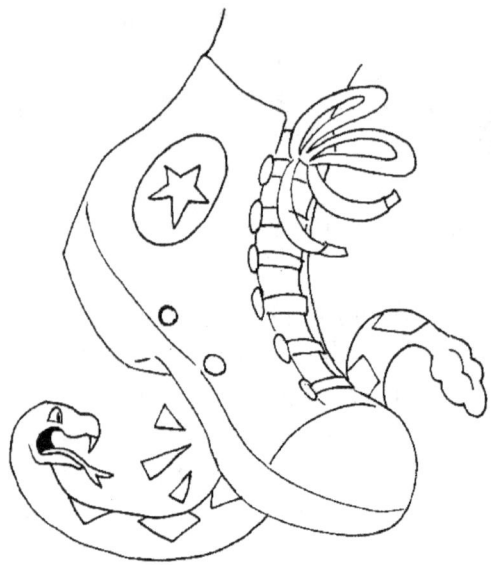

Snakes Alive!

Once upon a time, I stepped on a rattlesnake. It was a baby snake, but they can kill you just as quickly as a mature four-footer.

The sun rose as the dogs and I finished our walk. Both are snake trained to alert me when a snake is present. They did not alert me, but breezed past as if the snake was a rock. I will never nominate my dogs for genius grants.

My foot felt something wriggle, and I instinctively eased up before putting my weight down. The baby snake rattled, and I felt an immediate need to evacuate my bowels.

I stopped, putting just enough pressure to hold the snake in place but not enough to crush it. I had no way of knowing if it would strike or flee if I released it.

My *former* Prince Charming stood at the head of the driveway. "It's a rattler!" I said. "What should I do?" I wanted to be rescued.

"I'll put the dogs in the house," he volunteered. That is *all* he volunteered. He stood at the other end of the driveway. This Prince Charming, it seems, does not do snakes.

The tiny snake could twist its head just enough to bite my sneaker.

I was in a standoff with the rattler, with Prince Charming muttering something about how he needed to get to work.

They say when you are near a rattlesnake, stand still and it will eventually slither away. They never say what to do when *standing* on one.

I froze for a few moments, hoping someone would come to my rescue. Prince Charming studied the finches at the feeder. He jiggled his car keys.

I took a deep breath, crouched and ran as if my life depended on it. Which, by the way, *it did.*

The snake shot off into the desert and I ran straight into the house, tossing my fang-punctured sneaker in the washing machine.

Prince Charming drove off to work.

Once upon a time, I stepped on a rattlesnake. I came to my *own* rescue.

Fight Club

A wooden block sails past my head and slams into the shutter behind me. I duck, and just in time. I lock eyes with my granddaughter before she yells, "I was aiming for *him!*" She points to her brother.

I've never seen the movie *Fight Club*, but today seems as if I'm living it.

More yelling and screaming ensues as their parents mete out punishments.

Later, as my granddaughter and I draw chalk flowers on the back patio, a scream sends me to my feet. My older grandson runs toward me, clutching his side. Appendicitis? A fall from the slide? Fire ants?

"He *bit* me!" He points at his brother, who stares at the grass while the injured party lifts his shirt to show me the wound. It looks like a rabid skunk got hold of him.

Apparently, they allow biting in this Fight Club.

Once again, there is yelling and screaming, and I mete out punishments.

After dinner, we sit quietly in the playroom surrounded by dolls, action figures, cars, trains, and the tragic remains of a once proud warrior princess. Fight Club treated her cruelly.

"Stop it!" my older grandson screams at his little brother.

"Mine!"

"I'm playing with it!"

Both have a stranglehold on a wooden train. I flashback to earlier in the day and a wooden block. Before I can act, the train mysteriously whomps my younger grandson on the forehead. He falls back, too stunned to protest. I see a massive knot forming.

"It was an accident!" yells my older grandson.

The first rule of Fight Club is: You do not talk about Fight Club. The second rule of Fight Club is: You do not talk about Fight Club. The third rule of Fight Club is: Someone yells "Stop!", goes limp, or taps out, the fight is over.

Someone needs to teach my grandchildren the rules of Fight Club.

Siren Song

I stand for a second admiring my clean closets. I stuff the back of my car with out-of-fashion purses, 20-year-old coats, worn-out shoes, clothes I no longer wear (or no longer fit), and assorted odds and ends.

My closets are now organized and clean and the rest of the house breathes easier. All that's left is to carry them to the charity store.

Placing my hands on my hips, I stand for a moment as Queen of My Castle, Mistress of Clean, a solid member of the Order of the Organized. I wonder if God feels like this after a good rain.

I slam the back of the car shut and practically strut into the house.

I hunt down Pip, who has guessed it's time to go to the dog groomer. My house is clean now—nowhere to run and nowhere to hide.

Pip climbs into the car. I suspect he is thinking many bad words. I don't care—I am ruler of all I survey.

The charity store is next to the groomer, so I drag Pip (again, more bad doggie words) in for his one-hour appointment. I haul bag after bag, box after box into the charity store. I pause for a moment, hoping the attendant will congratulate me on my boldness and clarity. She smiles and hands me a receipt.

I complete my trifecta by getting the car washed. Clean house, clean dog, clean car. I am AMAZING!

I scan the horizon and there it sits, like the Sirens' rocky coast, HomeGoods—purveyor of all thing's household and at a *discount*. Like the ancient sailors, I can no more turn away than I can stop the rain.

I avert my eyes. But no living soul can resist that Siren song of tablecloths, hand towels, baskets (oh, the baskets!), dishes, and pillows (really, they are practically *giving* them away). Not to mention dog beds, rugs (a new rug really spruces up *any* room), and lamps that will instantly transform dark corners into welcoming havens of comfort.

Did I mention everything is at a *discount*, a *deep* discount?

Thirty minutes later, the back of my car is once more stuffed to capacity. I retrieve Pip, who pouts and tries to gnaw off the purple ribbon they tied around his neck.

Thank heavens I made all that room in my closets!

Be Beautiful

She is tall, blond, and *young*, wearing white jeans so tight you can practically map her veins.

I wander through the plant nursery on an almost cool day in early fall. The hideous desert summer heat fried many of my flowers and now it is time to refill my planters and pots.

This woman is so beautiful that I cannot help looking at her. She is the white equivalent of Beyonce. If I were to stand next to her, I would look like a hobbit.

She shepherds an older woman—a woman probably my age. I get a tiny thrill imagining White Beyonce being rude to her companion, but even from this distance, I can see she is kind and speaks softly. They point at various plants and laugh and smile.

I move to the other end of the pansies and select several lovely blue plants. I head to the geraniums. The endless days of searing heat turned mine into the geranium equivalent of tumbleweed.

Suddenly, White Beyonce is standing next to me. I *do* look like a hobbit.

She and her companion pick up a pink and white geranium—exactly the one I was reaching for.

"I'm so sorry," White Beyonce says, holding the plant out to me. "Were you reaching for this one?" Even her voice is beautiful.

I feel like a grubby serf next to the queen. Scuttling away, I mumble apologies.

Before I avert my eyes, I read the message on her white t-shirt.

Be Your Own Kind of Beautiful.

I want to hate her, but you can't hate this many-layered kind of beauty. She *is* her own kind of beautiful.

And I am still a hobbit.

Good-Time Party Girl

"You're having wine *again*?" Mom is staying with me for a few days while she recovers from surgery. "You drank wine *last* night."

"Yes. Yes, I am." I give myself a very large pour. "Care for a glass?"

She scrunches her face and toddles to the kitchen table. She scrunches her face a lot when she visits me.

She pokes my homemade chicken soup with her spoon. "Why is the chicken in strips?"

"I shred the chicken with my hands, so it comes out in strips." I plunk my over-large glass of wine on the table. "I even made the chicken broth from scratch." Like the fool I am, I wait for her to praise me.

"Campbell's cuts its chicken in chunks."

"That's because a machine cuts it."

There's that scrunchy face again. We finish the soup in silence.

"How about a funny movie?" If she's in front of the TV, I can't see the scrunchy face. I find *Spy* with Melissa McCarthy and leave her to watch it while I do the dishes. Her head whips around when she hears me laughing.

"That movie won the award for the most vulgar film of the year," she says. Again, with the scrunchy face.

My parents saved money all week so they could buy jug wine on the weekends. When Mom became single, bars were her second home.

At least once, the bar expelled Mom and my cousin for being too drunk. Say what you will about me, I stay sober enough so I can remain *in* the bar.

In high school, I woke up more than once to find one of Mom's friends passed out, face down, on the front lawn after a party. I did object when one of them threw up in my bathroom sink. Those ladies could out-party USC frat boys.

"That's your *second* glass of wine," Mom says.

"Yes. Yes, it is." I kiss her goodnight and take my *second* glass of wine to my bedroom and curl up with a book. Who's the good-time party girl now?

Of Potato Salad and Moon Men

My son and I climb into the almost-clean Uber. We've been at a zoo wine tasting fundraiser (Winos for Rhinos) and done a little more fund raising than perhaps we should.

"My name's Jerry," our driver says as he pulls away from the curb. We ask a few polite questions, which somehow leads to a lecture on potato salad. It seems Jerry's wife and he used to make the best potato salad on the planet.

"This one time, we flew our potato salad to an event. When we got there, they said they didn't have any rental cars," Jerry says. "I told them, I had to get this potato salad to the event. They still said they didn't have any cars." Jerry pauses to pull his car back into the correct lane.

"So, I gave the manager a taste of my potato salad." Jerry turns and smiles. The guy heading toward us honks his horn. "The manager said it was the best potato salad he'd ever tasted, and we had to get it to our event." Jerry turns around again.

At this point, I'd be happy if Jerry got me to *my* destination in one piece. The potato salad is on its own.

"So, the rental car manager gave me his own car. Told me to keep it all weekend. His own personal car." Jerry beams in the rearview mirror.

I turn to my son, and we shrug. "It might be safer if we drove ourselves," he whispers. I nod.

The driver next to us flips Jerry off. Jerry doesn't notice.

"Remember the moon landing?" Jerry asks. Before I can shush him, my son says, "Sure."

"What they didn't show you on the TV was all those little men who were there."

"Really?" I consider grabbing my son and bailing out at the next stoplight—if Jerry bothers to stop.

"Yeah, when Neil Armstrong landed, all these little space men who came to congratulate him surrounded them." The car swerves but Jerry never misses a beat. "NASA has the tapes, but they refuse to show them. Don't want to scare us."

Moon men are *not* what's scaring me right now. I grab my son's arm and he grabs mine. *I've lived a good life, but he's too young to go*, I think.

Suddenly, I am home. I practically weep with joy. My poor son still has another ten minutes listening to Jerry describe the moon men, but he texts later that he got home safely.

Maybe next time I raise funds for the rhinos, I will salute them with sparkling water.

Then again, probably not.

The Golden Girls

When my dog, Scout, snores, it's like fighter jets roaring through the room and then blasting you on the return trip.

If she's not snoring, Scout, my ancient cattle dog, snuffles and digs to get her bed just right.

She is an old dog, and I am an old woman. We are growing old together. It's like *The Golden Girls* with dog hair and kibble.

I type as the fighter jets roar through my office. Then the jets depart, and Scout hauls herself up on arthritic knees. She toddles over and begins rubbing her face along my pant leg, as if she's channeling the spirit of a kitty cat.

I know it sounds sweet, but she is an old dog and leaks fluids from every orifice. By the time she's done, my pant leg looks like the towel wipe of an NBA player.

At least I'm wearing long pants today. When I wear shorts, it's like being slimed in *Ghostbusters*.

I visit my doctor for my annual checkup and mention my arthritis is acting up. Every joint creaks these days like the wheels on a rusty cart.

"Let's try some meloxicam," she suggests. "It's a nonsteroidal and doesn't have many side effects."

I stare at her for a moment. Finally, I say, "My dog, Scout, takes meloxicam."

My doctor finds this wildly amusing. I do not.

She orders the medication and I head home to shaking foundations and sonic blasts.

I open the door and Scout toddles to me, her tail wagging. She rubs her head along my pant leg to tell me she loves me.

The Golden Girls never prepared me for this.

Lighting Up

Son of a biscuit! The buckles on my 2-year-old grandson's car seat will not quite fasten—another growth spurt.

I lift him out while I try to remember how to loosen the straps. I push. I pull. I stab buttons. I say bad words to myself. The straps don't budge.

The manual will tell me what to do! I pry it out from under the car seat just as the radio begins to play. My grandson pushed the button that would start the car. Lucky for me, he can't reach the brake pedal, or the car would start. When he figures that out, they'll find me flattened like a cartoon cat as my grandson races through town.

I page through the manual, which has 63 pages on how to install the car seat. So far, not one tells me how to loosen the shoulder straps.

Rap music blasts through my car. He's managed to change the radio station, a feat that takes me hours. He giggles when I look at him.

Suddenly, the back window wiper is swishing in time to the music. I've never been able to make that work and here it is practically ready for *Dancing with the Stars*.

Finally! I push the right button and the shoulder straps loosen. I now spend the next few minutes trying to capture my grandson and get him back in his seat. It's like trying to nab The Flash.

We both laugh as I pin him in the seat and fasten the buckles. I am exhausted. "Nana's car! Nana's car!" he says, clapping his hands.

I feel like it may soon be Nana's *coffin* if these escapades continue.

Grandson strapped in; I plop in the driver's seat. My dashboard looks like Chevy Chase's house in *Christmas Vacation*. One of the lesser bad words pops out of my mouth. I have no idea what any of these lights mean. Is my car safe to drive or am I in imminent danger of an explosion?

I start the engine and the car seems to run properly. I ease down the driveway and some of the lights disappear.

Once my grandson learns to put together coherent sentences, maybe he can teach *me* how to operate all these lights.

Staying Alive

If they're alive at the end of the day, then I've done my job, was my motto when raising my sons. Using each other for BB gun target practice, rocketing toys into space, jumping off roofs, cars, and anything else they could climb kept me on high alert 99% of their childhood.

I didn't *dare* drink alcohol in case I needed to make a dash for the emergency room. Polite society frowns on drunk moms who rush their kids to the ER.

They have their own families now and no longer need me to clutch car keys in case of a mad race to the doctor. Congratulating myself on a job well done, I relaxed the no drinking policy. *A lot.*

And then came China. That fascinating, frustrating festival of humanity we visited together. I envisioned a relaxing romp through the Chinese countryside with my boys. China had other plans.

At one of our first lunches, I sat next to my younger son as we feasted on Chinese delicacies after touring the Forbidden City.

I noticed my son's face turning red, and I assumed it was the stimulating table conversation. Suddenly, I realized his face was *purple*. Something in the Chinese food sparked an allergy, and the guides rushed us back to the hotel. He was fine, but we were both on high alert for the rest of the trip.

I still drank, of course. The guides would do any driving. As it turned out, they had to.

Midway through the trip, my older son woke up one morning vomiting every ten minutes for 16 hours. The guides rushed us to a Chinese hospital, where I discovered that the term *Chinese hospital* is an oxymoron.

Thanks to his brother, the doctor, my older son survived. He finally curled up in the hotel room and slept for hours. I went straight to my hotel room and ordered wine from room service.

Navigating China with my sons was much like navigating their childhoods—delightful periods of extreme joy tempered with bursts of terror.

I took my sons to China, and they were alive at the end of the trip.

I'll drink to that.

Forget-Me-Not

"Will you remember, Nana?" my grandson asks. We are discussing how early he can wake me in the morning. "Do you want me to write it on a sticky note and leave it by your bed?"

"I'll remember," I assure him.

"Maybe I should leave a sticky note anyway. Just in case."

"In case of what?" I am puzzled by his determination to leave me a note. "Why do I need a sticky note?"

"Because Dad is always telling us stories about how you forget things."

Sharper than a serpent's tooth is a thankless child. I turn to my older son. "You've been telling him how much I *forget*?"

"Not really," my son backpedals.

"Yes, you were." I glare at my son and his face turns red. My son glares at *his* son, who has an innocent look on his face but the devil in his eyes.

A crash at the other end of the house distracts us and I hurry to find my two youngest grandsons locked in a death grip over a toy horse. The WWF has nothing on these toddlers.

The screaming and crying escalate as I pry them off the horse and toss it into a closet. Their mothers retrieve and soothe them.

I retreat to my office to avoid the crying and yelling, mostly from the adults. I note an escalation in banging and voices but focus on my keyboard.

As I peck away on my computer, the house becomes quiet—silent, even. No yelling, no running, no banging of toys and cousins' heads, no noise at all.

The door to the garage flings open and my daughter-in-law says with a touch of impatience, "Nana, are you coming?"

"Coming where?"

"We're headed to dinner. Everyone's in the car."

Son of a biscuit, I grab my coat and shoes. I forgot.

The Light

I know everyone is already in the car waiting for me, but I can't help myself. The grandkids (and their parents) piled into the van, leaving on every light in the house. I go from room to room, flicking off switches.

I tell myself I am being a good custodian of the Earth, but deep down, I know I'm just being cheap. Ebenezer Scrooge is my spirit animal. I can hear the electric meter clicking away, piling dollar upon dollar on to my bill.

My son and his family are visiting from Houston, one of the rainiest spots on Earth. They beg you to use water in Houston—they have so much they practically give it away. I live in the desert, where you pledge your firstborn just to *get* water service.

Returning from our expedition, the grandkids pile into the shower where I hear the water run and run and *run*. They are laughing and playing, and I am beginning to steam. I'll need to hock my car just to pay the water bill.

I decide to say something, but then an image of my long-dead father appears in my head, snarling at me to turn off the lights. "You're burning money!" he'd yell.

Oh, no, I realize. What will I be doing next, scaring the neighbor kids by yelling at them to get off my lawn? Refusing to return their ball when it lands in my yard?

"Nana!" yells my granddaughter. "Come play with us!"

My first thought is, *I will get wet. I will get messy. It will ruin my hair.*

"I'm coming!" I say as I push back the wall of steam that fills the bathroom. "Nana is coming!"

A Walk in the Park
Part I

My grandchildren scramble up a boulder in the desert canyon behind my house. My son lifts the almost-four-year-old up and then gives me his hand to help me climb the smooth surface.

The grandkids scamper ahead, and I notice Pip is not with us. I look over the edge and he sits at the bottom. If he were human, he would tap his toes. He gives me the stink eye.

My sons explored this canyon constantly as boys and I always sent one of our dogs to protect them. They were big dogs, outdoor dogs, dogs that would tackle a grizzly bear. Pip thinks he's fierce when he tackles a stuffed squirrel.

My son peers over the edge at Pip and sighs. "Can't he just bushwhack around?" In his defense, Pip is a Swedish Vallhund and they, like me, have rather stubby legs. And Pip, like me, is no spring chicken.

"It's Pip." I shrug. My son mutters under his breath and climbs down, hoisting Pip up onto the rock. Pip is affronted at being plopped down like a common dog. My daughters-in-law named him Princess Pip for good reason.

The grandkids find a stream trickling along the sandy floor. They shoot up the narrow canyon, whooping like pirates.

Pip sits at the edge of the stream, looking at the water and then at my son. He does this several more times to make certain we humans understand his demands.

"I will *not* carry him across that!" My son stalks away, muttering, "He's a *dog* for heaven's sake!"

Pip now looks at me, then at the water. He looks at me, then at the water.

Everyone disappears around the bend. I step over the stream and lift Pip across. He shakes any microscopic drop of water off his coat and trots after the grandkids.

After all, we seniors with stubby legs must stick together.

A Walk in the Park
Part II

We've reached Abbey Falls in the desert canyon, where my sons used to scamper up and down the rocks. Today, three grandkids scramble up and down the boulders, shrieking with delight.

"Man, some of the stuff I used to do as a kid was *dangerous*," my son says as he lunges to catch his youngest.

My daughter-in-law and I decide to head back down before someone gets hurt. My son, ever the explorer, shoots up the side of the canyon.

"They've built a house there," I shout up at him. "We can't go this way."

"Yes, we can!"

I have a bad feeling about this. I help the grandkids and Pip bushwhack up the slope as cactus, palo verde, hackberries, and bursage pull at our clothes and scratch our arms. Pip is completely affronted and tries to retreat down the slope. I tug on his collar, and he trudges on.

The kids are tired. I'm tired. Pip is tired. My son leaps up the hillside like a goat. My daughter-in-law and I pause to catch our breath.

We scramble past a rock wall and suddenly find ourselves in a yard covered in immaculate artificial turf, rock gardens, and exquisite patio furniture. It could be featured in Architectural Digest. A very large sign says, *No Trespassing.*

"I told you there was a house here!" I hiss.

"Run!" says my son. Suddenly, two adults, three children, an old lady, and a disgruntled dog run, crouching as if we're in a combat zone. Pip keeps trying to pause and pee on their patio chairs.

I imagine a couple preparing brunch on a beautiful Sunday morning as they hear voices, looking out their windows, expecting to see the mountains rise behind them. Instead, a group straight out of *Hogan's Heroes* stumbles and dodges across their beautiful yard.

We hurl ourselves behind a pile of bricks covered in bushes and trees. Behind us, rocky cliffs. Ahead of us, a barbed wire fence, the driveway, and then the road and freedom.

"There's a gate!" I whisper. A big metal gate that is always closed against barbarians. And, apparently, wayward neighbors.

"Run for it!" my daughter-in-law commands. Several of us are bleeding from scratches, but we can't pause now for triage.

"Go!" says my son. He lifts the youngest over the barbed wire and then goes back to carry Pip. We dash down the brick driveway as if the hounds of hell are at our backs. For all we know, they might be.

We turn the corner, and the gate is open! With a final burst of speed, we escape onto the neighborhood asphalt, panting and holding our sides. I pause, sure I'm going to hear sirens.

"Let's do that again!" my grandson laughs.

Witchy Woman

The Harrison House stood on an overgrown lot, surrounded by ancient trees, vines running rampant, and assorted brambles and bushes. To get to the house, you walked along a narrow, dirt driveway. None of us dared even try, no matter how hard the other kids teased.

One Halloween, I stood at the bottom of the driveway as the wind rustled leaves and tree branches creaked. "Go on!" a tall boy said. "Don't be chicken!"

We were *all* chicken. Everyone knew she was a witch living in a house like that. Suddenly, a light appeared as she pushed open her front door. We ran like rabbits before a hound.

Many neighborhoods have a local "witch," an old woman living by herself with an overgrown yard and a short temper. I claim witches in my bloodline. My mother yells at any child who dares even *look* at her back patio.

I don't *want* to be a witch. I bake cookies for the neighborhood kids at Christmas. I smile and wave when I see them.

I have a long driveway, I'll admit, but I try to keep it from becoming overgrown.

But sometimes it does. When my son visited the last time, he pulled out a large plant that bloomed and died and was hanging across my driveway. He gave me that look that said maybe it's time to get a condo. I gave him the finger.

This morning, I woke up later than usual, realizing it was trash day. I grabbed a cup of tea, threw on a robe, and rolled my trashcan down to the street. My hair looked as if a crow nested in it overnight.

No one will see me, I reasoned, it's not even fully light yet.

Just as I rolled the can into place and prepared to dash back up my driveway, a bicycle appeared out of the gloom. I recognized the 12-year-old boy from next door.

"Good morning!" I called as cheerfully as I could muster after only one cup of tea.

His bike swerved, almost went off the road, and he sped up like a rabbit before a hound.

Frisky and 60!

"Frisky and 60!" the cup proclaims. I look from the cup to my buddy, OS, and back to the cup. I smile and cock my head.

The three of us usually give each other delightful gifts—scarves, bracelets, notecards, bookmarkers. After 25 years together, we know what we like.

An obviously *used* plastic cup with the number 60 printed all over it was not what I was expecting. Has OS fallen on hard times? Or worse, is this the beginning of senility for us all?

Pam cocks her head as well. At least I'm not the only one confused by the gift. The clatter of silverware and the voices in the restaurant suddenly seem a little too loud. We stare at the cup.

"It's you!" OS exclaims. "You're definitely *Frisky and 60!*"

"Thanks," I say. It's not a bad compliment, it's just not a slogan I planned on adopting. It makes me sound like an aged terrier fetching a stick.

"I'm passing it on to you!" she says, gesturing like Vanna White presenting the winning phrase.

Pam and I exchange looks that say, now we know which one of us is the first to wander down the senility highway.

"It's been my cup," OS says, "the one I use at home." She looks from one of us to the other. "My grandson said the other day, 'But Grandma, aren't you in your 70s?'"

She looks triumphant again. Pam and I glance sideways at each other. Should we tell her husband? Or does he already know? I vow to visit OS regularly in the retirement home.

"You're in your 60s!" she insists. "The cup now belongs to you!"

It's true, both my dear friends strode into their 70s several years ago. I'm still hacking my way through the 60s jungle, at least for a few more years.

I'm the slow one here, I realize. She's passing the torch from one decade to the next. This is an *honor*.

As my buddies smile at me, I am young once again.

You Say You Want a Revolution

"Twenty years ago, we had a toilet revolution in China," the perky Chinese guide informs us as we scramble through a former nuclear power plant.

A revolution? 'Cause I just went to use their revolutionary toilet, and it was a hole in the ground.

The Chinese love showing off their technological accomplishments. Guides get teary-eyed extolling the virtues of the Three Gorges Dam.

Chinese toilets, however, made no such technological leap. Most are holes in the ground. I admit that many of the tourist attractions now have some Western toilets available. Unfortunately, if a Chinese woman used it before you, she has climbed up onto the seat and squatted. Chinese women, it turns out, do not have precision aim.

Our tour guide warned us there wouldn't be toilet paper, so we came prepared with packages of tissues. What they didn't warn us about was the lack of soap at most bathrooms. The women in our group huddle together at each restroom stop, sharing tissues, wipes, and hand sanitizer. We ration them as carefully as Londoners did their food coupons during the Blitz.

The toilet revolution consisted of simply having *any* public toilets at all. Twenty years ago, it was common to see people squatting in the street because there were no facilities. Small children still do. Around Tiananmen Square, there are long trenches covered with grating. When there's a rally, the guards pull up the grating so everyone can squat over the trenches.

Western hotels have Western toilets, thank heaven. The St. Regis in Cheng Du had a Japanese toilet featuring heated seats, bidet and automatic flushing. Every time I entered the bathroom, the lid popped open like a dog jumping to greet its owner. I named mine Henry. My sons pried me away from it when it was time to leave.

Our tour bus stops at a rest area on our way to Guilin. The women in our group have become numb to the indignities of holes in the ground and no soap. We are toilet warriors now.

"Oh, my," the first woman through the door says.

"Good heavens!" says the next.

"*Hell*, no!" says the third.

Without discussing it, we turn away from the door and use the grass area behind the restroom. The men look away.

Our toilet revolution begins.

Smear Tactics

"I'm off for my annual checkup," Jamie says as we roll up our yoga mats.

"I hate all that poking and prodding," Lila says.

"And the *at your age* speech," adds Mattie.

"I have my checkup today, too," I realize.

"You're younger than us, though," Mattie reminds me. I silently congratulate myself on being the youngest of our group.

"More tests, more poking, more questions," Jamie says. "Except for pap smears. At least we don't have to do *that* anymore."

"What do you mean?" Lila snaps her head around. "They don't do pap smears on you anymore?"

"Mine doesn't," says Jamie. "Not since I turned 65."

"Does that mean we're so close to death now that no one *cares* if we get cancer?" Lila rears back her head.

"I don't mind," Jamie says. "I'm just glad I don't have to do it."

"I still get a pap smear," I offer.

"That's because you're *younger*," Jamie reminds me.

"Well, *I'm* going to fight for my right to have one," Lila says. "They're not writing me off so easily." She huffs out of the room.

I shower and head over to my doctor's office.

My doctor comes in and we discuss her daughter's wedding and our brilliant, beautiful grandchildren. We chat, she pokes and prods, and before I know it, I'm dressed and out the door.

I stride to my car, congratulating myself *again* for my youth and good health.

As I slide into my seat, I suddenly pause. Wait, a minute—something was missing from my exam. Several *very* bad words erupt from my mouth.

My doctor didn't do a pap smear.

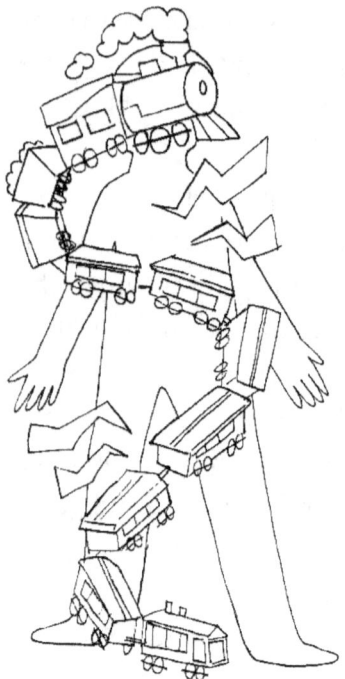

The Pain Train

The pain train tours my right hip this morning. I envision the locomotive building up steam and power as it chugs over the hilly and bumpy terrain of my gluteus maximus.

To get around some of those curves, the engineer must fully stoke those fires.

Yesterday, it stopped at the rail station by my right shoulder. Apparently, it is touring the right side of my body these days.

"The pain went from my left side to my shoulder and then down to my knee. Then it disappeared," says Mina.

She's lucky, her pain train has chugged off into the wild, blue yonder. Mine charges full steam ahead.

We call it the pain train because it moves mysteriously from one place to the next, always racing away just before the doctor can diagnose it. The engineer must be a sadistic gnome zooming from station to station, cackling with glee.

"I wish I knew how to close those stations," says Jackie. "Especially to my left knee."

Sometimes the train jerks from joint to muscle and then speeds on. Sometimes, it sits puffing and boiling in the station. It always dashes away before I can secure a diagnosis.

We finish lunch and head to our class on Broadway musicals. Julie brought her own cushion to sit on. I remember when I used to chuckle at old folks who carried their own cushion. Now I envy her.

The chairs are plastic, and I can feel the engineer feeding logs into the fires of the pain train. He is cackling louder with every minute my bottom rests on this nightmare of a chair.

The teacher finishes and we all stand up, groaning slightly. Julie scampers out the door like a teenager.

Once home, I sink into a hot bath, generously sprinkling in Epsom salts. Maybe, just maybe, I can drown the pain train's engine before it revs up to full steam in the morning.

I scroll through Amazon, searching for seat cushions.

Washed Up

My washing machine is on strike. It is one-and-a-half years old and flashes *E 21* at me.

Because a broken washer is not considered an emergency, I am forced to wait four days for a repairman.

Four days later, my house looks like the African plains dotted with termite mounds. Piles of whites molder in one room, while the darks stare gloomily in another. The delicates modestly reside in the closet.

By the time the repairman appears, I practically cheer and line his path with rose petals.

I hear clanking and muttering and poke my head into the laundry room.

"Any luck figuring it out?"

"Look in that plastic box."

Piles of soppy, gray matter that resemble something Oliver Twist would be forced to eat are in the plastic box.

"Looks like you've been washing rugs," he says.

"Yes, I have," I admit. I am suddenly wary, like someone who is being accused of a crime.

"Don't wash rugs. Too much stuff gets washed into the filter."

"Can I clean the filter?" I ask.

"It's under the motor. Gotta take the machine apart to reach it."

"I'm no engineer, but that seems like a *giant* design flaw," I say. He shrugs and continues putting my washer back together.

"How," I enquire, "am I supposed to clean my rugs?"

"Laundromat."

Silly me. I thought buying a washing machine meant you didn't *have* to go to the Laundromat.

He puts the washer's parts back in place and I give him a check for $133.

"No more rugs, now." He winks.

I stand for a minute, watching him leave. Before his truck has even exited the driveway, I pile bathroom rugs into the washer.

Gone with the Wind

"Pull your knees into your stomach," says my yoga teacher. "This is called the Wind Relieving Pose."

And boy howdy, is it. I struggle to contain substances yearning to break free. I'm not doing *that* in my class. Not with my buddies next to me. And there's no dog to blame this time.

I seem to spend an inordinate amount of time these days containing substances, both of air and liquid, inside my body. It's like I've become a dispensing machine for rude noises and embarrassing fluids.

"Down on your stomachs, please," the yoga teacher instructs. She moves us into Boat Pose, where I reach back and grab my ankles with my hands and rock back and forth *on my bladder*. At least three of us rise and dash to the restroom afterwards.

All the stretching and twisting can free other systems of the body, especially for vegetarians. They stay out longer when they scamper from the room.

"Are you doing your Kegel exercises?" my doctor asked last week.

"Yes," I tell her. Of course, I am—how else to keep the floodgates closed at this age? Some days, I'm just one bad sneeze away from adult diapers.

I remember my grandmother walking across the kitchen, little puffs of digested material emitting from her backside with every step. "Ooh, ooh, ooh," she'd twitter. It was adorable. It would most certainly *not* be adorable for me.

Thank heavens for modern medicine. Popping a Gas-X is routine these days.

"Let's do another round of the Wind Relieving pose," my yoga teacher says. I tuck my knees into my chest and squeeze. I realize too late—I forgot to take my Gas-X this morning.

Arrested Development

"Well, whatever you do, just don't get arrested," my mother says.

"Why? Because of my extensive rap sheet?" I am already regretting this phone call. "I am going to Machu Picchu and the Galapagos, for heaven's sake! Not on some world drug tour."

My mother is silent, but I know what she's thinking; Cousin Bec and I party too much. When her friends come to visit, Mom only allows them one glass of wine. Then the bottle disappears, and it remains unfound for at least another week.

What Mom doesn't understand is that after a second glass of wine, Bec and I fall asleep. The snoring, drooling kind of sleep.

With those encouraging words in my ears, I head off with Cousin Bec to our first stop, Lima, Peru. Over a second glass of wine, Bec and I tell our fellow travelers about Mom's parting words.

"You know what we should do," Roberta says, leaning in. "We should ask some policeman to pose for a photo of you two being arrested." Roberta is well beyond a second glass of wine, but we like her idea. "Handcuffed and leaning over a squad car."

"Ask her for bail money!" John laughs. "She just might end up paying for your trip!"

Of course, it is our second glass of wine, so Bec and I head off to our respective hotel rooms to dream of handsome policemen handcuffing us.

The next morning, we tour Lima's Spanish Colonial buildings, oohing and ahhing over gilded statues and towering ceilings. As we wander around Lima's main square, Roberta grabs my arm. "Look, policemen!"

We whisper and plan and Roberta is just about to ask one of them to arrest us. Suddenly even more policemen trot into the square and begin setting up barricades. I notice they are all carrying very large rifles and look as if they would like nothing better than to use them.

We all huddle around our tour guide, who whisks us into another fabulous colonial house.

A week later, Bec and I sit on our ship in the Galapagos. We have just returned from seeing land iguanas and giant tortoises on the island and massive marine iguanas on the beach.

Suddenly, the tour director asks us about our final destination and then scurries off to talk to the others. We set down our glasses of iced tea (Yes, iced tea. The bar doesn't open until five.) and discover Ecuador has given us 24 hours to get out of the country.

We were vaguely aware of the coronavirus's impact but felt safely cocooned in our world of sea lions and blue-footed boobies.

The ship races to the port and we are whisked out of Ecuador on a chartered flight.

At four in the morning, we struggle off the plane in Miami. We search out a Chick-fil-A and order breakfast sandwiches.

"You know," Bec say, "we may not have gotten arrested, but we sure as hell got ourselves deported."

Sorry, Mom. It was the best we could do.

Down the Toilet

I have never heard so much about toilet paper in my *life*. And I've lived a *long* life.

I was floating contentedly in the Galapagos when the Ecuadorian government and the coronavirus propelled me back to my country where the dominant form of currency evolved into toilet paper.

Toilet paper?

And it's a *respiratory* virus, not the kind where you actually need toilet paper.

"Do you want me to order you some toilet paper?" my thoughtful and kind daughter-in-law wrote while I sipped wine and swapped stories with my fellow Galapagos passengers.

"I think she's finally lost it," I say to Cousin Bec. "Why is she writing to me about toilet paper?" We laugh and speculate about what has finally pushed her over the precipice. Probably my son, we both agree.

I should have heeded her offer. By the time I return to the U.S., toilet paper is disappearing faster than nuts at a squirrel party. The clerk at Target informs me that when they get a shipment of toilet paper, it vanishes within 30 minutes.

When I was a child, people stocked fallout bunkers in case of an atomic attack. They piled in enough supplies to last them through the nuclear winter. I remember canned beans, bandages, and Velveeta cheese, but I don't recall floor-to-ceiling shelves devoted to toilet paper.

Wait a minute—my buddy Rhonda is texting. I see a plethora of exclamation points. She's at Target and, miracle of miracles, they've just received a shipment of toilet paper!

Gotta run!

Checking In

My phone pings with a message from my neighbor. She asks if I need anything during the quarantine.

"I can't remember," she writes, "if you have family in town."

I assure her I do, and we text back and forth about her children and keeping busy. She recommends a television series and I recommend a movie.

I thank her for checking in. We sign off and I return to the computer. Something tickles the back of my mind and I pause. Then it hits me. She was following the guidelines of this new age. She was checking on the *elderly*.

Son of a biscuit!

"Hey Mom," my son texts, "wanted to let you know most of the stores now have special shopping hours for people *your age*."

Son of a biscuit!

"I know," a friend writes, "you don't think of yourself as elderly, but you really *are*."

Son of a biscuit!

To add insult to injury, each day my gray hair asserts itself more and more. If this quarantine goes on much longer, I'm going to look like Granny on *The Beverly Hillbillies*.

I briefly contemplate using a sharpie to erase the gray freeway running down my scalp.

To distract myself, I look at photos from my recent trip to Machu Picchu and the Galapagos with Cousin Bec. I smile as I see photos of us clambering up and down the stone walkways of the Inca city.

I really should text Bec, I think. She's a few years older than me. After all, it's everyone's duty to check on the elderly.

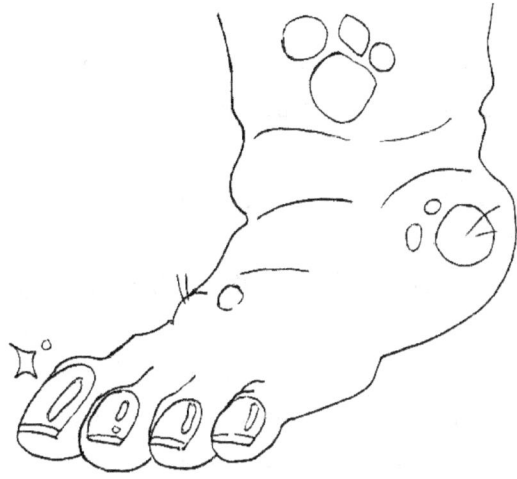

Nailed It

I dig the toenail clippers out of the bottom of a drawer and bend down. I have not cut my own toenails in twenty years, so imagine my surprise when I finally locate them and discover they are *hideous*. Troll-foot *hideous*. Hobbit-foot *hideous*.

Bending down, by the way, is a lot harder than it was 20 years ago.

All I can think is that the woman who regularly (until the quarantine began) dealt with these disgusting little piggies must be a saint. I never once saw her retch or jump back when presented with my toes.

And no one would have blamed her if she had.

I suspect her colleagues salute her as she heads toward me with clippers and a footbath.

I, however, am shuddering as I stare at the toes that used to be lighthearted and fun. Toes that could wear sandals without even a dab of polish. Young toes that boldly frolicked in sand and grass and water.

The kindest thing I could do for my fellow humans, I realize, is to wear socks the rest of my life.

But summer is coming, and the end of the quarantine is nowhere in sight. I owe it to the rest of humanity to attempt to camouflage these monsters with some cheery polish.

What I really need is spackle and a chainsaw.

I gamely begin snipping. I cannot even manage to get them straight across. My toenails now look like gravestones neglected for hundreds of years.

It takes many bad words and a pulled arm muscle but eventually I finish. I choose a nice, neutral color. All I can hope for is that no one will notice them.

Once I return to my nail salon, I vow that I am going to tip that woman a lot more.

Just in case this drags on, though, I'm going to buy a *lot* more socks.

Banking on It

I love my bank. The tellers all know my name and greet me when I arrive. It's the fiscal version of *Cheers*.

But now, because of quarantine, I cannot enter the bank. Banking is a matter for machines these days.

"I have some checks that I need to deposit," I tell Katy, the bank teller, over the phone. She is young and tries very hard to be patient with me.

She and I both know I could technically deposit those checks at a machine, but Katy also knows I will never master it. It will end in tears and bad words.

"Just fill out deposit slips and drop them in the night deposit box," she offers. "As soon as they're processed, I'll post them to your account."

Hope flutters in my chest. Open a drawer, put the paper inside and close the drawer. So simple, Katy thinks even *I* can do it.

Katy is wrong.

I confidently pull up to the bank. I wave to the staff and strut toward the night deposit drawer, clutching my checks and deposit slips.

It takes three tugs to get the drawer open. In my defense, I thought it would be like a mail slot in a door. Instead, I am confronted with a dome of solid metal and no discernable slot. Just a tiny slit that barely accommodates a piece of paper.

Luckily, I have Katy on speed dial. I can feel her sigh through the phone.

"I don't see the slot."

"Pull open the drawer all the way." Katy says.

"It's not really a drawer. It's a big hunk of metal."

"Just push it through the opening at the back," she says. I should nominate Katy for sainthood.

I take a deep breath and push the envelope. It *sticks*, halfway. I can't get it to go forward and I can't pull it back.

I begin to panic and bang on the metal dome.

"Just a minute," Katy says. I hear locks turning and doors opening. A few minutes later, Katy's voice rises through the dome. "Just close the drawer," she says, "and I'll catch the envelope."

I slam the drawer harder than I intended. "Got it!" Katy shouts.

"How *are* you?" I yell down through the dome. I hope for news of her children and the rest of the bank staff.

"Considering I am lying on my back at the bottom of the night deposit drawer with envelopes dropping on me, I am doing okay."

I pause in horror. Then I turn to run. "Thank you!" I shout as I leap into my car and pull away.

I just might have to switch banks.

Nail Biter

My fingernails were one of the first casualties in the war on the coronavirus.

People are on life support. People are *dying*.

So, it seems completely ridiculous for me to lament the gradual deterioration of my fingernails.

But I do.

And let's not even discuss doing my own nails. It's been weeks and I still can't get the old polish off. My nail gal puts that stuff on to *stay*.

Then, I hear of someone who broke the rules—a city mayor, no less.

Beaumont, Texas Mayor Becky Ames somehow got her nail salon, The Nail Bar, to open just for her. But someone looked through the window and took her picture.

Busted!

She made a mistake, she says. She was wrong, she says. The district attorney is investigating her.

But her nails look *fabulous.*

So, is there a fingernail underground? Could I really convince someone to encase my fingers once more in pink powder and shellac? I am an elderly woman (as society, and my sons, so often remind me) so there's very little I can do about my appearance without committing major surgery.

But, until recently, I could have beautiful nails. Now they look like they belong to an elderly woman who sculpts cement.

I dream of digits soaked in beautiful little bowls, someone massaging my hands, picking a color from hundreds of samples, cuticles trimmed to perfection. And walking out with my hands and head held high.

Mayor Ames is not my hero. But I am just a bit jealous.

Living the Dream

"You are living the dream!" My insurance agent beams at me.

My head whips around. Is she talking to someone else?

"You are on your own!" she adds. We are updating my insurance needs for the coming year.

I am puzzled because she's *married*. She was just mentioning her husband.

I start to remind her of the time there was a packrat floating and bloated in my wildlife pond and I fished it out *on my own*. It slid into various pieces and I'm not at all sure I retrieved every last bit of fur or internal organ. I still have flashbacks.

Or the time a rattlesnake took up residence in one of my drains. I dealt with that *on my own*.

Or the time I was so sick I could barely crawl out of bed to retrieve some stale crackers *on my own*.

"You don't have to pick up anyone else's dirty laundry," my insurance agent says. She's still beaming as if she imagines me living in a princess castle. She has no idea about entering a party *on my own* or buying a car *on my own*.

"You don't have to cook for anyone!"

Okay, I'll admit, that's pretty sweet.

"You get to do *what* you want, *when* you want!"

I remember last night when I crawled into bed after a day of chasing my toddler grandson all over the house. I poured a glass of wine and started a new novel with the dogs curled up around me.

Oh, I realize. Maybe I *am* living the dream.

About the Author

Photo by Dan Hartman

After forty-two years of marriage, Susan's husband suddenly developed the annoying habit of dating, and she found herself single. She turned to wine, cereal, family, wine, friends, wine, and her writing.

While raising her family, Susan reported and freelanced for newspapers in Colorado, edited business publications, and contributed essays and articles to magazines. As grandchildren began appearing, she wanted to focus on being Nana, but life had other plans. Instead, stumbling through the first months of being abruptly single, Susan saw that life required cushioning if she was going to thrive. Humor smoothed out those rough edges.

Susan now lives her best life chronicling her foibles and those of her sons, friends, grandchildren, and dogs. She also enjoys a glass or two of good wine.

About the Illustrator

Photo by Melissa Luzader

Claire Luzader draws in all mediums, from freehand to digital, and aspires to be a professional 2D animator. In addition to creating art, Claire loves reading and animals. She is a student living in Phoenix, Arizona.

Other Titles by Susan Luzader

Note from Susan Luzader

Word-of-mouth is crucial for any author to succeed. If you enjoyed *Wine and Cereal: Volume Two*, please leave a review online—anywhere you are able. Even if it's just a sentence or two. It would make all the difference and be very much appreciated.

Thanks!
Susan Luzader

We hope you enjoyed reading this title from:

www.blackrosewriting.com

Subscribe to our mailing list – *The Rosevine* – and receive **FREE** books, daily deals, and stay current with news about upcoming releases and our hottest authors.
Scan the QR code below to sign up.

Already a subscriber? Please accept a sincere thank you for being a fan of Black Rose Writing authors.

View other Black Rose Writing titles at www.blackrosewriting.com/books and use promo code
PRINT to receive a **20% discount** when purchasing.

www.ingramcontent.com/pod-product-compliance
Lightning Source LLC
Chambersburg PA
CBHW072200070526
44585CB00015B/1233